Advanced Studies in E-Commerce

Advanced Studies in E-Commerce takes a fresh and global viewpoint to E-Commerce development. It encompasses such issues as the basic concepts and principles of E-Commerce, the industry chain of E-Commerce, the security management of E-Commerce; the architecture of E-Commerce; the analytics of E-Commerce; and some cutting-edge topics of E-Commerce.

Yong Pan

Trust Management in the Chinese E-Commerce Market

Based on the Perspective of the Adverse Selection

西安交通大学出版社
XI'AN JIAOTONG UNIVERSITY PRESS

Springer

Yong Pan
School of E-Comm. and Logi. Mana.
Henan University of Economics and Law
Zhengzhou, China

Advanced Studies in E-Commerce
ISBN 978-981-97-1114-7 ISBN 978-981-97-1115-4 (eBook)
https://doi.org/10.1007/978-981-97-1115-4

Jointly published with Xi'an Jiaotong University Press
The print edition is not for sale in China Mainland. Customers from China Mainland please order the print book from: Xi'an Jiaotong University Press.

This Springer imprint is published by the registered company Springer Nature Singapore Pte Ltd.
The registered company address is: 152 Beach Road, #21-01/04 Gateway East, Singapore 189721, Singapore

Contents

Chapter 1
Introduction

1.1 The Topic Selection

In a nutshell, adverse selection[1] refers to the choices that consumers make when they are at an information disadvantage. Adverse selection theory was put forward by Professor George A. Akerlof, one of the Nobel Prize winners in economics in 2001. It mainly studies the influence of asymmetry of product quality information on market efficiency. Because this theory is based on the 'lemon' problem,[2] it is also called 'lemon market' theory. Through his 'lemon market' model (also called Akerlof model), Akerlof proved the consequence of information asymmetry: adverse selection caused by 'lemon' problem reduces the efficiency of market transactions. Take the used car market as an example. The seller knows the true quality of the car, but the buyer doesn't know it, only knows the average quality of the car, so he is only willing to pay the price according to the average quality.

However, if he does this, the seller with higher quality than the average level will withdraw from the transaction, and only the seller with lower quality will enter the market. That is to say, only low-quality used cars are sold, but no high-quality used cars are traded. As a result, low-quality used cars squeeze high-quality used cars out of the trading market. This means that the used car market shows low transaction efficiency.

Akerlof's analysis of market and information asymmetry is of far-reaching significance. His model can be used to explain the emergence of many social systems that offset the negative effects of information asymmetry, deepening our understanding

---

[1] As for the translation of the concept of adverse selection, some works and documents also translate it as 'adverse selection', 'adverse selection' or 'adverse selection'.

[2] 'Lemon' is a general term for 'old car' and 'defective car' in American colloquial language. After Akerlof [1] made a classic analysis of the 'lemon' market (used car market), 'lemon' became an economist's proxy for low-quality products (fake and inferior products). And 'lemon market' is also extended to 'defective market'. Because 'adverse selection' is caused by the 'lemon' problem, economists make no special distinction when using these two concepts.

Y. Pan, *Trust Management in the Chinese E-Commerce Market*,
Advanced Studies in E-Commerce, https://doi.org/10.1007/978-981-97-1115-4_1

of real market phenomena and changing economists' understanding of market operation mode. He also proposed and explained ways and means to reduce and avoid adverse selection. 'Lemon' theory has become a classic theory of microeconomics on the analysis of information asymmetry. However, Akerlof's analysis is for traditional markets or traditional businesses. So, what will happen in the internet-based online market?

In fact, when people rejoice in the convenience and high efficiency brought by the Internet, they have to face such a fact at the same time: that is, because the Internet gets rid of the limitation of time and space, it creates the virtuality of Internet trade, and the adverse selection problem ('lemon problem') caused by information asymmetry in Internet trade may deteriorate because of such external reasons. However, from the existing literature, the theoretical research on adverse selection and 'lemon market' model in the Internet market is a weak link in economics and management, and there are few papers specializing in this problem.

Therefore, the question that this paper pays attention to is: Is there a 'lemon' problem in the Internet market? If it exists, what are its characteristics and laws? How to build a 'lemon market' model in the Internet market. What is the particularity of adverse selection in China's Internet market? More importantly, how can we reduce or avoid adverse selection in the Internet market?

1.2 The Research Background

There are two main reasons for taking adverse selection in Internet trade as my research direction:

1.2.1 The Need for Theoretical Research

Since 1990s, with the development of IT industry, especially the rapid expansion of the Internet, Internet economy has become the theme of new economic activities. The rapid development of information technology is changing the behavior of enterprises and consumers and the relationship between them.

The development of practice must be reflected in theory. In fact, with the development of IT industry, Internet economics, e-commerce economics, information economics and other related disciplines are also extremely active. However, on the whole, the theoretical research still lags behind the practice: on the one hand, there are many new economic phenomena along with the Internet economy, and economists need more time and energy to observe and study it; on the other hand, the original

Table 1.1 Foreign articles specially discussing the Internet 'lemon' problem (adverse selection)

Author	Thesis title	Names of magazines and publishers	Date
S.Y. Choi, D.O. Stahl, A.B. Whinston	Quality Uncertainty and Market Efficiency: 《The Economics of Electronic Commerce》(Chapter 4)	Macmillan Technical Publishing, Indianapolis	1997
John H. Huston Roger W. Spence	Quality, Uncertainty and the Internet: the Market for Internet lemom	American Economist, Vol. 46, Issue 1	2002

Source Collation of this study

theory lacks convincing explanations for many problems in practice.[3] Among them, the research on the 'lemon' problem in the Internet market is like this.

Undeniably, e-commerce provides us with a search method with unlimited advantages. The effectiveness of Internet technology and services has changed the search behavior of potential buyers.[4] Existing software can enable consumers to search for all information about price and quality. This prompts us to think about such a question: Will consumers in the Internet market get complete information? Is there still information asymmetry in e-commerce market? Furthermore, there is still a 'lemon' problem in the e-commerce market? However, we have observed the fact that although the wide application of the Internet has greatly improved the information asymmetry, the 'lemon' problem (adverse selection) on the Internet is actually strengthened because of the virtuality of the Internet [2]. For example, the variability and differentiation of Internet product content, the difficulty of identifying the identity of Internet traders and the subjectivity of market participants' evaluation of Internet product utility will all cause the 'lemon' problem in the Internet market.

Although the 'lemon' problem in the Internet market has also attracted the attention and interest of some economists, from the existing literature retrieval, there are few papers specializing in this problem (see Table 1.1), and accordingly, the depth and breadth of the papers are also very limited. As Huston and Spence [3] pointed out, 'It is surprising that so far, only a few economists have published articles on the' lemon 'problem in the Internet market in mainstream economic journals'. Therefore, it can be said that the 'lemon' problem in Internet trade has not attracted enough attention from mainstream economists, and its theoretical research is a weak link in economics and management.

In addition, from the development of the 'lemon market' model itself, the current domestic research on this issue is more just as an economic analysis thought, a

[3] Carol pointed out that the existing Internet economics still lags behind practice, 'so that there has never been a yearbook to summarize its past laws and analyze its future trends' (Review on the Book, The NFAIS Yearbook of the Information Industry: Information Processing & Management Vol. 31, 1995).

[4] Economic analyses of relevant countries and international organizations (Zerdick et al. 2000) [2], policy reports [5, 6, p. 6, 9] (OECD 1997, ch. 2) and market research (Alba et al., 1997) all agree that Internet technology generally reduces search costs.

Table 1.2 Comparison of Internet search and purchase by Internet consumers

Products or services	Online search (%)	Online purchase (%)
Air ticket	35	19
Book a hotel	29	13
Computer hardware	24	13
Automobile	31	1

Source MccLea and Wheat [4, pp. 146–153]

general description of the original model, but also lacks evolutionary research and promotion of the Akerlof model, especially the research on the Akerlof model of the Internet market has basically not been involved.

Therefore, from the perspective of the development of information economics itself, we also need to pay enough attention to this problem.

1.2.2 The Needs of Internet Economic Practice

The US *Fortune* magazine once published an article titled 'Internet is a lemon'.[5] This article reveals the 'lemon' phenomenon in the Internet market, and compares the Internet search behavior of buyers with the purchase behavior (as shown in Table 1.2).

It shows that even in the United States, where the business environment is very good, people still hold a wait-and-see, cautious and even skeptical attitude toward the quality of Internet products. More people just use the Internet to search, and the proportion of actual buyers is relatively low, especially for car sales. According to the annual survey report of automobile purchase released by the American Consumers Union (CU) in 2001,[6] although nearly two thirds of users make purchase decisions through the Internet, only 1.5% of users actually buy automobiles through the Internet. According to the survey, 42% of users are uneasy about the safety and information of Internet purchase. This fact shows that under the virtual environment of the Internet, the information asymmetry faced by people has not disappeared or declined because of the emergence of the Internet, on the contrary, it is still serious in some cases. FBI statistics show that the number of Internet fraud cases in the United States has increased dramatically in recent years. In 2002, more than 48,000 Internet fraud cases were sued by American consumers to prosecutors, which is three times that of 2001. Losses from Internet fraud in 2002 amounted to $54 million, compared with $17 million the previous year.[7] It is precisely because of the 'lemon' problem in Internet auction transactions that serious Internet fraud has occurred, which has

[5] See MccLea and Wheat [4, pp. 146–153].

[6] Quoted from: http://www.marketingman.net/wm35/502.htm.

[7] http://www.people.com.cn/.

brought certain losses to society and economy. The United States has set up an organization IFCC (the Internet Fraud Complaint Center)[8] to analyze and deal with these problems. According to IFCC, the total annual loss of these complaints is as high as $3.2 million, and the average loss per complaint is $776.

In addition, according to the survey results of the 12th Statistical Report on Internet Development in China (2003/7) by China Internet Information Center,[9] the proportion of Internet users who choose shopping as their main purpose and implement transactions in China only accounts for 0.2% of the total number of Internet users. The main reason for this situation is that Chinese netizens have a great degree of distrust of the quality of Internet products. This shows that the 'lemon' problem in China's Internet market is serious, and it may even affect the development of China's e-commerce. Therefore, while people are intoxicated with the convenience of modern internet technology, they can't ignore the information asymmetry brought by Internet virtuality and the Internet 'lemon' problem caused by it. It is of practical and realistic significance to study the adverse selection in the Internet market for the development of China's Internet market.

1.3 The Purpose and Significance of the Research

The main purpose of this study is: taking the adverse selection (Internet 'lemon' problem) in the Internet market as the research object, taking the Internet 'lemon market' model as the basic starting point, combining theoretical analysis with empirical analysis, studying the mechanism of product quality uncertainty in Internet market, exploring the development law of adverse selection in the Internet market and putting forward strategic suggestions for Internet management and Internet marketing on this basis.

Today, with the rapid development of Internet economy and e-commerce, this study has both theoretical and practical significance.

1. The research on Internet adverse selection can provide academic accumulation for the development of traditional economics and traditional management. From the development of Internet economics, it has experienced the development process of The Economics of Network Industries → Internet Economics → The Economics of Information Infrastructure → The Economics of Electronic Commerce [7]. This development track shows that the research hotspot of network economy is determined by the stages of Internet development: the first three stages are the problems that must be solved after the construction of

[8] Located in Morgantown, West Virginia, the US Internet Fraud Complaint Center is led by the Federal Bureau of Investigation (FBI) and the National White Collar Crime Center, which provides intelligence on white-collar crime trends for judicial authorities. The purpose is to give consumers and companies a strong complaint channel for online fraud incidents (website: http://www.ifccfbi.gov/).

[9] Quoted from the website of China Internet Information Center (website: http://www.cnnic.cn/).

Internet infrastructure, such as resource allocation and pricing, and the economic characteristics of Internet; the latter is the requirement of theoretical research put forward by the rapid development of e-commerce practice.[10] However, traditional economics and management theory in explaining the lag of Internet economy, which has become the consensus of academic circles. Therefore, it is the need of theory and practice to form Internet economics facing digital economy as soon as possible. The efforts made in this study will strive to contribute to this.

It should be pointed out that the laws of economics and management applicable to today's Internet economy actually come from traditional economics and traditional management to a great extent. As Shapiro and Varian [8] point out, 'If you observe it properly, many aspects of the Internet economy can be found in the old economy'. Therefore, this study not only includes the application and inheritance of traditional theory, but also includes the questioning and revision of it.

2. The research of Internet adverse selection can make us grasp the operation law of human Internet market better and analyze the prospect of consumption and sales behavior of buyers and sellers.

   It is an indisputable fact that human production and consumption behavior will be greatly changed due to networking, but how to adapt to the transformation and change of this way is a problem to be solved. This paper will explore the influence of Internet adverse selection on the consumption and sales behavior of participants in the Internet market.

3. The research on Internet adverse selection can provide some decision support for Internet management and social regulation.

   In traditional economic theory, there are 'market-oriented' methods and 'non-market-oriented' methods to solve the 'lemon' problem. Solving the 'lemon' problem in the Internet market still depends on these methods, but they have different characteristics. Especially for our country, with the rapid expansion of the Internet, many problems and difficulties will be in front of us, and the 'lemon' problem is one of them. If there is a lack of research on the inherent laws of Internet behavior, the management will be weak and ineffective. Therefore, this study can provide a decision-making basis for the management problems in the development of Internet.

4. The research on Internet adverse selection can help enterprises get out of the misunderstanding of Internet marketing.

   Some enterprises believe that Internet consumers are only sensitive to price, and only low prices can win consumers; other enterprises believe that Internet

---

10 The research on Internet economy in the United States can be clearly divided into two stages: from 1993 to 1997, it was the first stage of Internet economy research, which mainly took the Internet itself as the research object, and studied the resource allocation and pricing, the compatibility between Internet and standards and the externality of Internet in the construction of Internet infrastructure; from 1998 to now as the second stage, this research focus began to turn to the commercial application of Internet, mainly focusing on e-commerce and its related economic, technical, legal, social and political issues (Chen Yaogang, Jiang Yanzhang, 《Current Situation and Trend of American Internet Economy Research》, 《Economic Dynamics》, No. 12, 2000).

brands are Internet advertisements. In fact, this is a misunderstanding. The Internet 'lemon' principle will tell us: Because of the existence of Internet 'lemon', the price of Internet products and Internet advertisements, as a signal of product quality, play a limited role in the Internet market. To solve the fundamental problem, we should also take advantage of the Internet characteristics and adopt various ways to improve consumers' loyalty and satisfaction with Internet products.

1.4 Research Methods

The main research methods used in this paper are as follows:

1.4.1 Model Analysis

Theoretical model is the basic point of analyzing problems in economics and management. This study constructs a mathematical model on the basis of theoretical analysis, with a view to revealing the development law of adverse selection in Internet trade, abstracting the essential characteristics of the Internet 'lemon' and making theoretical analysis on this basis. The main mathematical methods used in this paper include game theory and statistics, and the related results are analyzed and verified by CAS (Complex Adaptive System) modeling method.

1.4.2 Literature Analysis

Because the Internet 'lemon market' model and Internet adverse selection theory are still in the field that mainstream economics and management basically have not set foot in. Therefore, there are few papers about the 'lemon' problem in Internet, but the existing papers about the 'lemon' problem in the traditional market can provide us with the context of studying this problem and provide the necessary theoretical background materials for this study. This study attaches great importance to the role and value of existing literature.

1.4.3 Case Studies

Whether the theoretical model of this study is correct or not needs the support of practice. In addition, choosing representative things for case anatomy can obtain fresh first-hand information. Case analysis is very important and irreplaceable for the new research field of 'lemon' problem in Internet market.

1.4.4 Collection and Analysis of Internet Data

It is a very quick and effective method to investigate samples by using Internet. The Internet data used in this research mainly comes from the information published by existing commercial websites (such as eBay) and relevant authoritative websites (such as, China Internet Network Information Center [CNNIC]).

1.5 Architecture and Content

1.5.1 Logical Clues and Research Framework

The logical clue of this study is: putting forward the adverse selection (Internet 'lemon' problem) in Internet trade → tracing back the theory of adverse selection → establishing the theoretical model of Internet adverse selection → solving the theoretical thinking of Internet adverse selection → analyzing and exploring the solutions → proposing countermeasures. Subsequent chapters will be developed with this logical clue. The research framework of this paper is shown in Fig. 1.1.

1.5.2 The System Structure of This Paper

In addition to the introduction, there are eight chapters in this paper.

The first chapter mainly discusses the research background, research objectives, research methods and research framework of this paper, and briefly describes the innovation of this paper.

The second chapter mainly summarizes and analyzes the theoretical origins of adverse selection and 'lemon market' model. This chapter starts with Professor Akerlof's pioneering work and makes an analysis and explanation of Akerlof's classical model (and translates Akerlof's classical papers into Appendix 1 of this thesis). This paper defines the concept of adverse selection and analyzes the characteristics, functions and theoretical value of the classical 'lemon market' model. As a literature review, this study summarizes the evolution track and the latest progress of the 'lemon market' model and points out that the research on Walrasian equilibrium under adverse selection, the essence of market equilibrium and non-market system will still be the focus of economics in the future, and the development direction of 'lemon market' in the future should expand from physical market to Internet market.

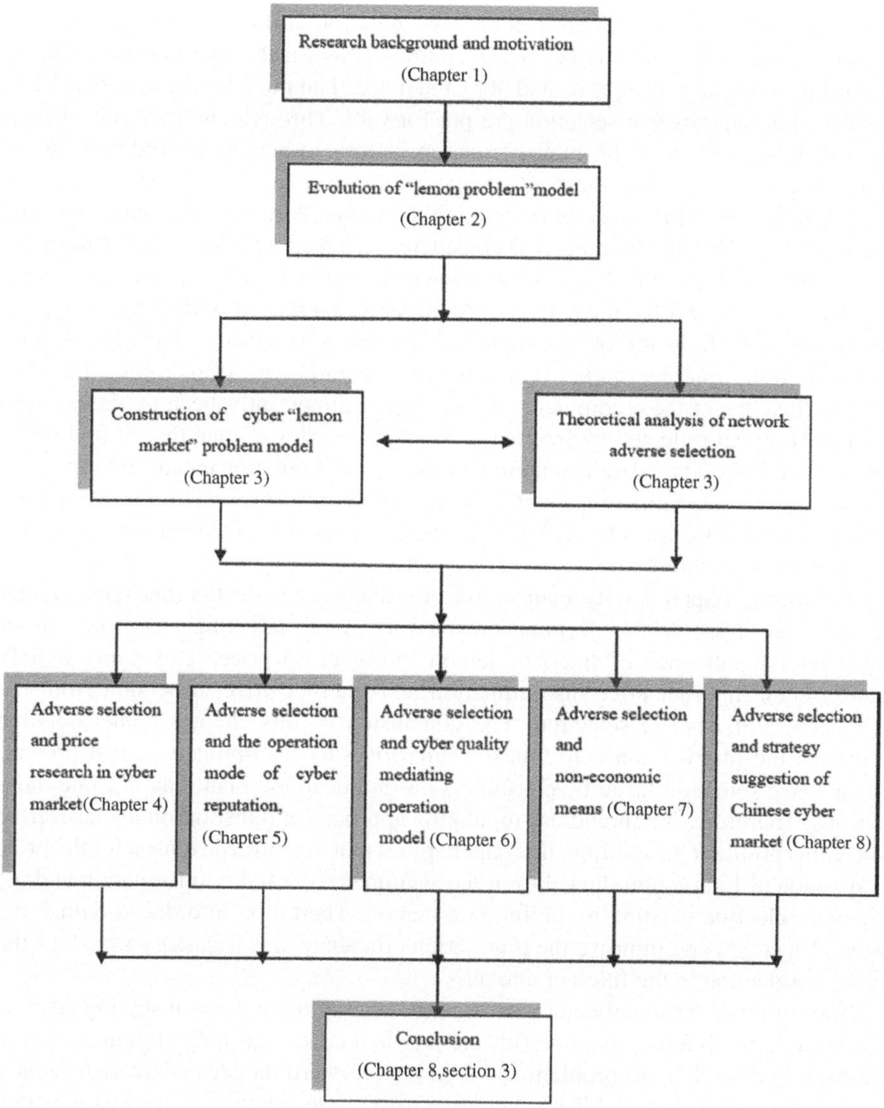

Fig. 1.1 The research framework of this work

The purpose of the third chapter is to provide a basic point of theoretical analysis for the following chapters. In this chapter, firstly, the causes of adverse selection in the Internet market are analyzed, and the Internet 'lemon' problem is described. Then, on this basis, the mathematical model of adverse selection in the Internet market is constructed and verified. As a generalization and extension of the theoretical model, this chapter analyzes the relationship between Internet market and physical market under adverse selection and puts forward the conditions of 'equilibrium separation' and 'market segmentation' between the two markets. Finally, according to the conclusions provided by the theoretical model, the theoretical ideas to solve Internet adverse selection are put forward. Through analysis, this chapter points out that because the Internet market is easy to achieve equilibrium at the low price level, it means the decline of welfare level in market transactions and the failure of spontaneous coordination in the market. Although the emergence and rapid development of e-commerce is considered to reflect the advantages of information environment and imply the substitution of traditional market, due to the serious adverse selection problem existing in the Internet market, it will have an adverse impact on the efficiency of transactions. Therefore, trying to reduce the 'lemon' problem in the Internet market is an inevitable requirement for us to give full play to the efficiency of the e-commerce market. More importantly, because the strength of quality signal reflected by Internet product price is lower than that of traditional market, we should pay special attention to the role of reputation means, intermediary means and non-economic means in solving Internet adverse selection. At the same time, compared with the physical market, the Internet market calls for the emergence of market coordinators.

The fourth chapter mainly analyzes the price behavior in the Internet market under adverse selection. While affirming the Internet price marketing mode, this paper analyzes the influence of Internet 'lemon' problem on price. This paper mainly analyzes the Internet price discrimination and Internet price dispersion from the perspective of adverse selection. The conclusion of this chapter points out that although the Internet can help Internet enterprises to discriminate against pricing, the adverse selection faced by consumers has not decreased but may become more serious. Therefore, we should use reputation approach and institutional approach to solve this problem. In addition, this paper argues that the intrinsic reason for the price dispersion of Internet products lies in the asymmetry of quality information and the adverse selection existing in the Internet market. Therefore, in order to reduce the price dispersion and improve the transaction efficiency, it is necessary to reduce the adverse selection in the Internet market.

The fifth chapter mainly analyzes the influence of reputation on solving adverse selection in the Internet market. This chapter first constructs a reputation operation model based on 'lemon' problem and then puts forward the idea of Internet reputation management and establishing Internet trust mode. The main conclusion is that although it is more difficult to establish one's own reputation in the Internet market than in the traditional market, this does not mean that it is impossible to establish the reputation of enterprises or products in the Internet market. This paper puts forward the concept of Internet 'reputation chain' and puts forward the viewpoint of 'reputation transfer' and 'brand extension' from traditional market to Internet market. This paper argues that Internet enterprises should recognize their own 'reputation chain', implement the strategies of 'reputation transfer' and 'brand extension' and use the methods of leasing reputation and co-branding to improve their reputation.

The sixth chapter analyzes the influence of Internet quality intermediary on solving adverse selection. This chapter constructs a quality intermediary model based on 'lemon' problem, and on this basis, puts forward the idea of using quality intermediary to solve Internet adverse selection. It is pointed out that the mechanism of 'information overflow' is a decisive reason to ensure the Internet quality and solve the 'lemon' problem. The larger the quality distribution of Internet products, the more quality intermediaries are needed. Therefore, as long as the new transaction costs can increase the welfare level of the whole society, effective intermediaries will still exist for a long time in the era of Internet economy.

In the seventh chapter, this paper analyzes the role of non-economic means in solving Internet adverse selection. Through the analysis of a game model of product quality, this paper explains the function and influence of non-economic means on solving adverse selection, points out that institutional factors such as non-economic means are of special significance to solving Internet adverse selection and discusses some methods that may be used as non-economic means, including legal means, administrative means, morality and trust.

The eighth chapter analyzes and studies the adverse selection in China's Internet market. After analyzing the general principle of adverse selection, this paper analyzes and observes the 'lemon' phenomenon and its performance in China's Internet market with the consumer behavior of Chinese netizens as the breakthrough point. This paper argues that as far as China's Internet market is concerned, the adverse selection faced by consumers is more serious. This is because the factors affecting the 'lemon' problem in China's Internet are special, including the acceptance of Internet information space, the consumption psychology of 'following the crowd' in Chinese traditional behavior, the negative demonstration effect of some non-standard websites, the rampant counterfeiting, the imperfection of relevant legal system, the weakness of consumers' power, etc. Relevant data also illustrate this point, so this problem must be paid attention to by us. This paper puts forward some strategic suggestions on eliminating or reducing adverse selection in China's Internet market. These suggestions include: (1) Fully understand the influence of adverse selection ('lemon' problem) on the development of e-commerce. (2) Technical means should obey the creation of value chain. (3) Implement the organic combination of Internet marketing and traditional marketing. (4) Implement the strategy of third-party intervention. (5) Give full consideration to China's national conditions. (6) Get out of the misunderstanding of Internet marketing. (7) To provide legal protection for solving Internet adverse selection.

1.6 Main Nnovations

The innovations of this paper mainly include:

1. This paper constructs 'lemon market' model in Internet market (or Internet Akerlof model) and takes it as the basic theoretical model to analyze the adverse selection problem in Internet market. Although economists after Akerlof

extended the 'lemon market' model, these extensions are still aimed at the traditional physical market, and the premise in the model is only relaxed to the difference of consumers' preference for quality among buyers. Based on the virtual nature of the Internet, this model relaxes the presupposition of this model to the difference in product quality preference between buyers and between buyers and sellers. In the process of building the model, this study uses von Neumann-Morgenstern expected utility function and considers the influence of continuous quality distribution of Internet products on market equilibrium. The Internet 'lemon market' model established in this study is not only the inheritance and expansion of the existing 'lemon market' model, but also the development of a new field.

2. Based on the basic theoretical model, this paper makes a preliminary analysis of the substitution between e-commerce market and traditional market. It is considered that with the quality uncertainty, the persistent adverse selection problem is induced, and a 'separated' equilibrium may appear between the e-commerce market and the traditional market. However, with the decrease of Internet 'lemon', the substitution of e-commerce market for traditional market will be enhanced. Therefore, trying to reduce the 'lemon' problem in the Internet market is an inevitable requirement for us to give full play to the efficiency of the e-commerce market.
3. From the perspective of Internet adverse selection, this paper analyzes the strategy of 'price discrimination' in Internet marketing and the phenomenon of price dispersion in Internet market. This paper analyzes the adverse selection problem in the Internet 'price discrimination' strategy and puts forward some suggestions on how to avoid this problem. At the same time, the author puts forward a new explanation for the phenomenon of price dispersion in the Internet market and thinks that the internal cause of this phenomenon lies in the adverse selection in the Internet market.
4. Based on the Internet 'lemon' problem, this paper constructs a reputation operation model in the Internet market, puts forward the concept of Internet 'reputation chain' and puts forward the viewpoint of 'reputation transfer' and 'brand extension' from traditional market to Internet market.
5. Based on the Internet 'lemon' problem, this paper constructs the operation model of quality intermediary in the Internet market, analyzes the necessity of the existence of Internet quality intermediary and thinks that the quality intermediary, as the third party, plays a particularly important role in eliminating Internet adverse selection, and it should and will exist for a long time.

References

1. Akerlof GA (1970) The market for 'lemon': qualitative uncertainty and the market mechanism. Quart J Econ 84(3):488–500

2. Alba, Joseph, John Lynch, Barton Weitz, Chris Janiszewski, Richard Lutz, Alan Sawyer, Stacy Wood. (1997). Interactive home shopping: incentives for consumers, retailers, and manufacturers to participate in electronic marketplaces. J. Marketing 61 (July) 38–53
3. Axel Zerdick, Arnold Picot, Klaus Schrape, Alexander Artope, Klaus Goldhammer, Ulrich T. Lange, Eckart Vierkant, Esteban Lopez-Escobar, Roger Silverstone (2000) Strategies for the Digital Marketplace, Springer.
4. Choi SY, Stahl DO, Whinston AB (1997) The economics of electronic commerce. Macmillan Technical Publishing, Indianapolis
5. Huston JH, Spence RW (2002) Quality, uncertainty and the Internet: the market for cyber lemom. American Economist 46(1):50–60
6. MccLea B, Wheat A (2000) The Internet is a lemon. Fortune 13:146–153
7. OECD (1997) Business-to-consumer electronic commerce: survey of status and issues. Head of Publication Services, Paris, OECD/GD(97)219. http://www.oecd.org/dsti/sti/it/ec
8. OECD (1997) The economic and social impact of electronic commerce: preliminary findings and research agenda. Head of Publication Services, Paris, OECD, OECD code 931999001lP1. http://www.oecd.org/dsti/sti/it/ec
9. OECD (1997) Business-to-Consumer Electronic Commerce: Survey of Status and Issues, Paris: Head of Publication Services, OECD/GD (97) 219 (http://www.oecd.org/dsti/sti/it/ec.)
10. Rong C, Xiaowu G (2001) Overview of the development of network economics. Economist 5:114–118
11. Shapiro C, Varian H (2000) Information rules: strategic guidance of network economy. Renmin University of China Press, Beijing, Trans. Zhang Fan
12. US Department of Commerce (1999) The Emerging Internet Economy II. Secretariat on Electronic Commerce, US Department of Commerce, Washington, DC. http://www.ecommerce.gov

Chapter 2
Adverse Selection, 'Lemon Market' Model and Related Literature Review

As a theoretical preparation for the study of adverse selection in Internet market, the main purpose of this chapter is to analyze the origin and development process of adverse selection theory and 'lemon' problem and summarize the related literature.

2.1 Introduction: Information Asymmetry and Adverse Selection

As the introduction of this chapter, we first define and analyze the asymmetry of information, the concept of adverse selection and the relationship between them.

2.1.1 The Asymmetry of Information

Asymmetry of information refers to the uneven distribution of market information between the two sides of the transaction. Professor Akerlof is a pioneer in the field of information asymmetry. He proved that 'if information asymmetry is very serious, it may limit the function of the market, and in extreme cases, the whole market will not exist'.

Regarding the research on the role and significance of information asymmetry in economic theoretical analysis and Akerlof's contribution, the Bulletin of Nobel Prize in Economics of Royal Swedish Academy of Sciences in 2001 pointed out,[1] 'Akerlof pointed out a very important fact: in many markets, sellers have more information about product quality than buyers'. 'There is information asymmetry in many markets: one buyer or seller often has more information than the other. Borrowers

[1] Translated from Nobel Foundation website (http://www.nobel.se/).

Y. Pan, *Trust Management in the Chinese E-Commerce Market*,
Advanced Studies in E-Commerce, https://doi.org/10.1007/978-981-97-1115-4_2

know their repayment potential better than lenders, business managers and boards know the future of enterprises better than investors, and customers know their accident risk rate better than insurance companies. The effective operation of a market economy requires sufficient common information between buyers and sellers'. The bulletin pointed out that 'the three award-winning economists discussed the problem of information asymmetry from the fields of product market, labor market, insurance and capital market, and pointed out that the market system needs to be improved and designed. This is a major breakthrough in traditional economics.[2] Their research reveals the core issues of contemporary information economy and lays the foundation for the theory of asymmetric information in market economy'.

2.1.2 *The Concept of Adverse Selection*

The concept of Adverse Selection originated from the insurance market [22]. In the insurance market, adverse selection refers to the situation that is unfavorable to the insurer in the insurance contract due to the asymmetry of information between the insured and the insurer. The essence of insurance is that most people raise funds to spread the risks of a few people. Therefore, through scientific actuarial methods, insurers know more about overall risks than policyholders, while policyholders know more about individual risks than insurers. In this way, as far as a certain insurance is concerned, people with high risks are more likely to enter the insurance, while people with low risks are less likely to enter the insurance. A person who is in good health is rarely willing to take part in life insurance, while a person who is in poor health or suffering from illness is willing to take part in this insurance. And this situation is unfavorable to the insurer. In view of adverse selection, on the one hand, the insurer can reverse infer the potential risks of the insured according to the total amount of insurance invested by the insured, collect the relevant information of the insured to understand the insured subject matter and weaken the information asymmetry between them as much as possible. On the other hand, it can further standardize the signing principle of insurance contract. And before signing the contract, strictly implement the principles, its purpose is to prevent the insured from making profits from the insurance.

The Royal Swedish Academy of Sciences[3] explained and described adverse selection in its press release: 'At a given price, sellers know the true quality of products, buyers don't know, only know the average quality of products, so they are only willing to pay the price according to the average quality, but in doing so, sellers with higher quality than average will withdraw from the transaction, and only sellers with lower quality will enter the market. That is to say, only low-quality products are sold,

---

[2] Professor Akerlof also won awards from A. Michael Spence and Joseph E. Stiglitz, who used asymmetric information theory to study labor market and capital market, respectively, and expanded and perfected adverse selection theory.

[3] See the Nobel Foundation website (http://www.nobel.se/).

but no high-quality products are traded, and the result is that low-quality products squeeze high-quality products out of the trading market. Such a process is adverse selection'. 'Adverse selection hinders normal and beneficial transactions, or in other words, Adam Smith's "invisible hand" is not always effective, and the market does not automatically tend to equilibrium-this is different from the principle described by traditional economics that we firmly believe'.[4]

Adverse selection is explained in *The New Palgrave Model of Economics*[5] as 'examining a market in which products of different quality are exchanged. Both buyers and sellers grade products of different quality according to the same method, but only the seller knows the quality of the products he sells. At best, the buyer can only perceive the quality distribution of products sold before. Buyers can't distinguish between good and bad goods, and bad goods are often sold together with good goods. Adverse selection illustrates this kind of market'.

From the previous definition of adverse selection, we can see that adverse selection comes from the asymmetry of information. The adverse selection described and analyzed by Professor Akerlof is mainly aimed at the quality information in the product market. As long as there are quality differences, there will be adverse selection behavior, which is caused by the 'lemon' problem in the market because consumers have to make reverse choices because of the disadvantages of quality information. Therefore, we can say that the essence of adverse selection comes from the difference of information—adverse selection exists not only in the product market, but also in any market with information asymmetry.[6]

2.2 The Origin of Theory: Adverse Selection Theory and 'Lemon Market' Model

Akerlof's contribution lies in introducing information asymmetry into our analytical perspective, thus laying the foundation for the new Keynesian economics that emerged in 1980s. More importantly, he not only put forward a method to reduce and avoid adverse selection, but also provided us with a basic perspective method to analyze problems. In order to analyze the Internet 'lemon market' and establish the Internet 'lemon market' model, we first make an analysis and interpretation of Akerlof's classical theory and classical model. One thing needs to be pointed out is that at present, the theory in China only stays in a general description of its ideas, and there is still a lack of in-depth study of the original model.

[4] See the Nobel Foundation website (http://www.nobel.se/).

[5] Eatwell et al. [10].

[6] For example, Myerson in (Game Theory: Analysis of Conflict Cambridge, Mass.: Harvard University Press, 1991) called 'problems caused by participants' incorrect reporting of information' 'adverse selection'.

2.2.1 'Lemon Market' Model and Adverse Selection: Akerlof's Classical Theory and Interpretation

Professor Akerlof's classic theory is embodied in his paper *'Lemon' Market: Quality Uncertainty and Market Mechanism* published in American *Quarterly Journal of Economics*,[7] which won him the Nobel Prize in Economics. We can express the analysis process of Professor Akerlof's [1] classic thesis as 'putting forward ideas → proving models → illustrating examples → explaining institutions → drawing conclusions'. In order to better understand the inherent meaning and influence of adverse selection theory, especially the 'lemon market' model, we will make an analysis of this paper, respectively:

2.2.1.1 Hypothesis: Put Forward Ideas

In the first part, 'Introduction', Akerlof first points out that the theme of his analysis is the relationship between quality and uncertainty and points out that different grades of products are an interesting and important issue in market theory. He pointed out that on the one hand, the paper tries to explain many important institutions in the labor market through the analysis of the relationship between quality differences and uncertainty, on the other hand, it tries to explain some statements such as 'business behavior in underdeveloped countries is difficult', especially on the costs of dishonesty, structure of money markets, insurability intentions, liquidity of durables and brand-name products, as examples and applications of this theory.

Akerlof pointed out that in most market environments, because buyers usually cannot observe the specific quality of individual commodities, buyers often use the average statistical value of the market as their basic understanding of commodities. Under this premise, according to the principle of utility maximization, the seller is encouraged to operate low-quality goods to maximize the income; however, the economic significance of the transaction growth of high-quality goods in the whole market is greater than that of individual sellers, and there are differences or contradictions between the overall interests and individual interests. As a result, the quality of traded goods and the market size will be degraded.

Finally, Akerlof pointed out that he can illustrate and analyze this idea through the example of automobile market and pointed out that the purpose of using this example is mainly to better understand this idea through concrete examples, but not to ensure complete equivalence with reality.

[7] Akerlof [1].

2.2.1.2 The Construction and Analysis of the 'Lemon Market' Model

In the second part, Akerlof takes the used car market as an example to establish his analysis model and discusses the market operation mechanism under the condition of asymmetric and uncertain quality information. This part is the core theory part. In order to be more logical and rigorous, Akerlof discussed it with three sub-topics:

1. Car Market. In the used car market, even 'new' cars may be inferior quality cars. Therefore, Akerlof divides the cars appearing in the used car market into four categories: 'new' cars and 'old' cars, while 'new' cars and 'old' cars can be good cars or bad cars (called 'lemons' in America). Although a single buyer in the used car market does not know whether the cars he buys are good cars or 'lemons', he can know the probability of their appearance. Assuming that the probability of a good car is q, the probability of 'lemon' is $(1 - q)$.

   Akerlof pointed out that when the car owner uses the car for a period of time, he will have a new judgment on the quality of the car, that is to say, he will give the car a certain probability value to judge whether it has become a 'lemon', and this new judgment will be more accurate than his original judgment. Thus, there is an asymmetry of available information: the seller has more information about the quality of the car than the buyer. However, good cars and sub-cars must be sold at the same price—because it is impossible for buyers to distinguish between good cars and sub-cars. In this way, the owner of a good car will not sell his own car. This is not only because he can't get the real value of this car, but also because he can't get the value of the new car he expected.

   In order to better illustrate this problem, Akerlof compared Gresham's Law[8] as a metaphor and pointed out the difference between these two phenomena: second cars drive out good cars because they are sold at the same price; similarly, bad money drives out good money because they have the same exchange rate. However, the second car can be sold at the same price as a good car because the buyer can't know whether the car is a good car or a second car, which the seller knows. However, in Gresham's theorem, both buyers ademand for cars as followsnd sellers can probably distinguish bad money from good money.
2. Asymmetric Information. Akerlof assumes that the demand for used cars depends on two variables—the price p of used cars and the average quality μ of used cars entering the transaction, and the demand function is $Q^d = D(p, \mu)$; the supply and average quality of used cars depend on the price of used cars, that is, there are $\mu = \mu(p)$ and $S = S(p)$; in equilibrium, for a given average mass, the demand for used cars should be equal to the supply, that is, $S(p) = D(p, \mu(p))$. When the price of used cars falls, so does the quality, which may eventually lead to no transaction at any price level.

   Akerlof used utility theory to construct its model.

   First, suppose there are two groups of market traders: the first group of traders and the second group of traders. Assume that the utility function of the first group

[8] Gresham's law refers to the phenomenon of 'bad money driving out good' in currency circulation. It was named after British businessman Thomas Gresham (1519–1579).

of traders is:

$$U_1 = M + \sum_{i=1}^{n} x_i$$

where M is the quantity of consumer goods other than automobiles, x_i is the mass of the first automobile and n is the quantity of automobiles.

Similarly, the second set of utility functions constructed by Akerlof is:

$$U_2 = M + \sum_{i=1}^{n} 3/2x_i$$

In order to continue the research, Akerlof assumes that both groups of traders pursue the maximization of expected utility. At the same time, it is assumed that the first group of traders owns N vehicles with mass x and obeys uniform distribution between [0, 2], while the second group of traders has no vehicles. In addition, the price of 'other goods' M is regarded as a unit.

Suppose that the first group has total revenue Y_1 (including revenue from selling used cars) and the second group has total revenue Y_2. The demand for second-hand cars is the sum of the demand for second-hand cars by two types of traders. In this way, we get the first group of traders' demand for cars as follows:

$$D_1 = Y_1/p \qquad \mu/p > 1$$

$$D_1 = 0 \qquad \mu/p < 1$$

Since it is assumed that the mass of automobiles is evenly distributed, the first group of supplies to automobiles are:

$$S_2 = pN/2 \qquad p \leq 2$$

The relationship between average quality and price is:

$$\mu = p/2$$

Similarly, the market demand of the second group of traders is:

$$D_2 = Y_2/p \qquad 3\mu/2 > p$$

$$D_2 = 0 \qquad 3\mu/2 < p$$

And the supply is:

$$S_2 = 0$$

Thus, the aggregate demand function $D(\mu, p)$ is:

$$D(\mu, p) = Y_1/p + Y_2/p \qquad p < \mu$$

$$D(\mu, p) = Y_2/p \qquad \mu < p < 3\mu/2$$

$$D(\mu, p) = 0 \qquad 3\mu/2 < p$$

Comparing the relationship between supply and demand, it is obvious that there will be Walrasian equilibrium only when the price satisfies $3\mu/2 < p$. However, since the average mass of a car offered at a price level of p is $p/2$, there is no transaction at any price level: despite the fact that at a certain price between 0 and 3, the first group of traders are willing to sell their car and the second group of traders are willing to buy at that price, which has little practical significance.

This part is the core part of the 'lemon market' model. We can better illustrate and explain Akerlof's analysis process and conclusions with a diagram (as shown in Fig. 2.1).

In the graph, ray $S(\mu = p/2)$ expresses the average quality of automobiles in the market, and is also the decision-making will and basis of the supplier; the lower right of ray $D(\mu = p)$ and the lower right of ray $D(\mu = 2p/3)$ are the decision boundaries of the demander. Obviously, the only intersection of supply and demand boundaries can only be $p = 0$ and $\mu = 0$, that is to say, only at this point can Walras equilibrium occur. But this equilibrium means that the actual

Fig. 2.1 Walrasian equilibrium of 'lemon' markets

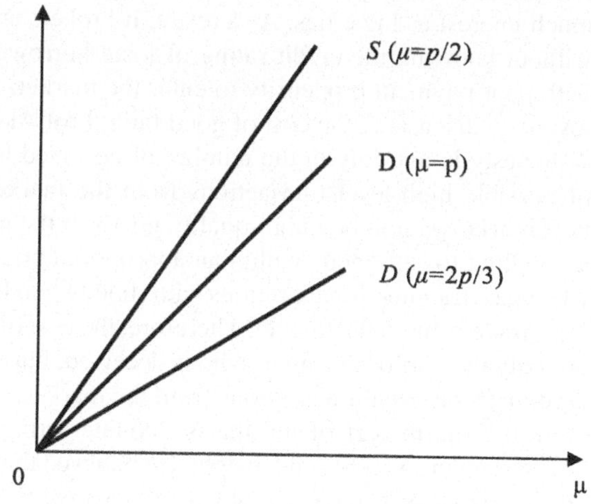

trading volume is zero, which has no practical significance. As a result, the whole market collapsed.
3. Symmetric Information. In this part, Akerlof assumes that all buyers and sellers have complete information, so that cars of different quality levels in the whole market can be sold at different prices.

Through the logical analysis of the above three parts, Akerlof proved his hypothesis with strict mathematical derivation, thus laying the foundation of 'lemon' theory.

2.2.1.3 Examples and Explanations: Verification of the 'Lemon Market' Model

In the third and fourth parts of the paper, Akerlof validates the 'lemon market' model.

In the third part, Akerlof explains the importance and universality of information asymmetry in practice with the title of 'Example and Application', thus verifying the 'lemon' theory and explaining it with this theory. These examples include Insurance, The Employment of Minority, The Costs of Dishonesty and Credit Market in Underdeveloped Countries. When discussing these issues, Akerlof uses a lot of data, charts and introductions. By discussing these market mechanisms similar to the used car market, this paper points out the great influence of so-called 'honesty' and information transparency on the economy. For example, in the insurance market, due to the asymmetry of information, it is difficult for the elderly over 65 years old to buy personal medical insurance, even if the premium is increased. In the job market, employers of some jobs are reluctant to hire minorities, not because of racial discrimination, but because of profit maximization, because race can show education level. Akerlof particularly emphasized the adverse selection in developing countries. For example, in India's local credit market in 1960s, money lenders demanded twice as much interest as big cities. As a result, if brokers arbitraged between these markets without knowing the credit rating of local borrowers, the risk attracted borrowers with poor payment propensity to enter the market, and brokers also suffered heavy losses. In discussing the cost of good faith, Prof Akerlof pointed out that the cost of dishonesty is not only in the number of deceived buyers, but also in the expulsion of possible high-level transactions from the market. Although there are potential buyers who want to buy high-quality goods in the market, and there are sellers who are willing to sell goods within an appropriate price range, the emergence of those who make fraudulent transactions with shoddy goods has driven legitimate and legitimate traders out of the market. Therefore, the cost of fraudulent transactions includes not only the part of the buyer who is deceived, but also the loss caused by expelling legitimate and legal transactions from the market.

In the fourth part of the thesis, 'counteracting institution', Akerlof expressed another important profound insight. He believed that many market mechanisms actually appeared to solve the problem of asymmetric information, because economic entities have strong motivation to offset adverse selection related to market efficiency. Here he lists several offset systems: providing guarantee in the transaction; let consumers identify by establishing brands; establish reputation and provide certified service records by setting up chain stores. In addition, education and labor market have their own 'brands'. This part also validates the 'lemon' theory and explains these market systems with this theory.

2.2.1.4 Conclusion

In the last part of the article, 'Conclusion', the author summarizes the full text. He pointed out that '"good faith" is very important. Informal and unwritten guarantees are the prerequisite for guaranteeing transactions and production. If these guarantees are vague and uncertain, business travel will encounter difficulties-as described by Gresham's theorem we have summarized'.

As for the application prospect of adverse selection theory, as Akerlof himself pointed out at the end of the article, the analytical tools used in the paper 'do explain many economic systems and will actually become a more important aspect of analyzing uncertainty'.

In fact, this prediction has come true now. The analytical method adopted by Akerlof has formed a classic literature on how economic systems can reduce the consequences of asymmetric information. The fact that his paper won the Nobel Prize in Economics 30 years after its first publication fully illustrates this point.

2.2.2 *The Theoretical Value of Adverse Selection Theory and 'Lemon Market' Model*

The adverse selection theory (or 'lemon principle') founded by Akerlof has very important theoretical value. Akerlof illustrates adverse selection with profound theoretical significance with popular and common examples. Its contribution to economics is that it reveals the information asymmetry phenomenon existing in many markets and deepens our understanding of the real market phenomenon. It tells us that the effective operation of a market economy requires enough common information between buyers and sellers. If the information asymmetry is very serious, it may limit the market function, cause the inefficiency of market transactions and even lead to the failure of the whole market.[9] It should be pointed out that although Akerlof takes old cars as the research object to analyze adverse selection, in fact, new

[9] In a later paper, 'The Economics of Caste System and Bad Competition and Other Sad Stories' (1976), Akerlof made a more systematic and comprehensive discussion on the replay of information asymmetry in different environments such as caste system, working conditions in factories and revenue sharing system. He used explanatory examples to prove that some variables called 'indicators' can provide important economic information to enhance efficiency, but they can also plunge the economy into an equilibrium that is harmful to society [3].

cars also have similar information problems, but old cars are more obvious. Not only cars, but almost all goods have more or less information problems. In his model, the old car is just an example, which is used to represent all the information asymmetry situations to explain the model. What Akerlof wants to analyze is all transactions with asymmetric information. Moreover, his analysis is rigorous and standardized, and a general model is established.

The basic ideas and basic perspective methods embodied in Akerlof's classic papers are of great theoretical value. It has brought us very important enlightenment to establish the adverse selection theory in the Internet market and the 'lemon market' model in the Internet market:

2.2.2.1 The Adverse Selection Theory Denies the Hypothesis of 'Complete Information'

Traditional microeconomics has two basic and common hypotheses: one is the hypothesis of 'economic man', that is, economic behavior individuals are rational people who make decentralized decisions; the second is the hypothesis of complete information, that is, both parties in the market have the same information, that is, the hypothesis of 'symmetric information'. In the analysis of market problems, this is a very important assumption. Only under this condition, the contract reached by both parties is perfect and the market result is efficient. Its purpose is to demonstrate the principle of 'invisible hand'. However, the real economic activities pose a severe challenge to the traditional theory. In fact, as Akerlof pointed out, in a market full of inferior goods, due to the serious information asymmetry between buyers and sellers, the result may be 'the inferior wins the superior', which leads to 'Market Failure' and even the serious consequences of complete market collapse. Akerlof's model reveals two conclusions that are contrary to traditional economics: (1) Under the condition of asymmetric information, the market may be inefficient. The conclusion of Akerlof model tells us that although some buyers are willing to pay high prices for good cars, the 'invisible hand' of the market does not transfer good cars from sellers to buyers. According to the theory of traditional economics, under the regulation of market, supply and demand can always meet the wishes of buyers and sellers at a certain price. (2) This kind of 'market failure' has the characteristics of 'adverse selection', that is, only defective products are left in the market, that is, 'bad money drives good money'. Akerlof's theory makes us understand that the root of this result is information asymmetry, which changes the angle of our analysis of problems and changes many 'common sense' conclusions.

Akerlof's academic contribution has gone beyond a simple theory. His analysis of information asymmetry and his demonstration of the conclusion of market failure have shaken the theoretical basis of neoclassicism. His viewpoint of 'approximate rationality' is also the basic perspective for us to analyze the behavior of Internet market.

It should be noted that the emergence of any theory has to go through a certain process, which is precisely illustrated by the recognition of Akerlof's adverse selection theory by theoretical circles. In fact, the bumpy process of Professor Akerlof's paper publication also illustrates the impact of his paper on mainstream economics.[10] Professor Akerlof attributed the bumpy experience of his paper to two aspects. First, orthodox economists at that time worried that the introduction of information factors into economics would change the stability and uniqueness of equilibrium; second, the writing style of the article is completely different from the popular rigorous expression style (without using the common mathematical language).

2.2.2.2 Adverse Selection Theory and the 'Information' Role of Price

Traditional economics and management generally think that the role of price is multiple, and among these roles, it emphasizes its 'information' function. For example, according to economic theory, price plays at least two roles in the decision-making process of consumers: one is the allocation role, and the other is the information role [21]. In the research on the role of price 'information', scholars also think that consumers' perception of product price is a good indicator of quality [9, 25]. In addition to economists, management scientists also look at the role of price from the perspective of product marketing. For example, Johnson (1985) think that the role of price in consumers' evaluation of product schemes is not single. They point out that the price paid by consumers for products will lead to the reduction of their wealth; in addition, they also believe that price can convey consumers' information about product quality, and this role gives price the nature of a product 'attribute'.

However, the 'lemon market' model shows that the root of market failure lies in the dual identity of market price: it should not only express the average quality level of automobiles in the used car market, but also become an equilibrium transaction price that makes supply equal to demand in the market. In the market with asymmetric information, the price actually shoulders the dual task of 'killing two birds with one stone', which it cannot be competent for. This is also the root of the function failure of the used car market. Finally, the market can only enter the vicious circle of adverse selection.

The above process can be illustrated in Figs. 2.2 and 2.3. Figure 2.2 shows that the average quality of used cars increases with the increase of the price of used cars. It shows that in an asymmetric information environment, commodity quality depends on price—which is contrary to 'quality determines price' in traditional economics. Figure 2.3 shows the supply and demand curve of the used car market. The supply

---

[10] Akerlof's classic paper was completed in 1967, and its publication was postponed because it was rejected by three authoritative economic journals. The American Economic Review says: We don't publish trivial things like this. The Journal of Political Economy commented that the articles were too universal to be authentic. The Review of Economic Studies rejected it on the grounds that the issues discussed in the article are too insignificant. Finally, after many twists and turns, it was finally published in the Quarterly Journal of Economics, which immediately aroused great repercussions [4].

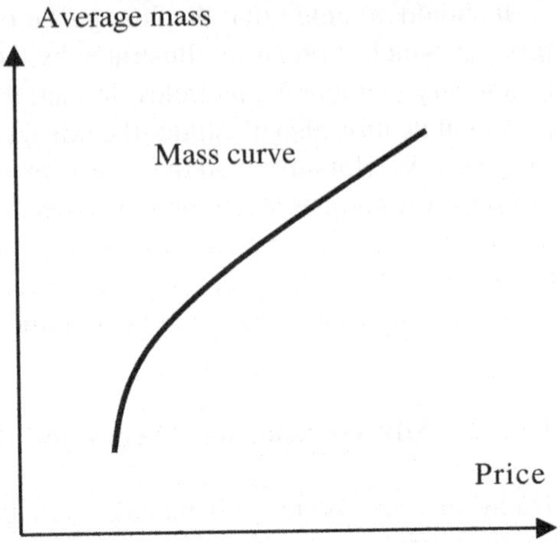

Fig. 2.2 Relationship between market price and average quality of used cars

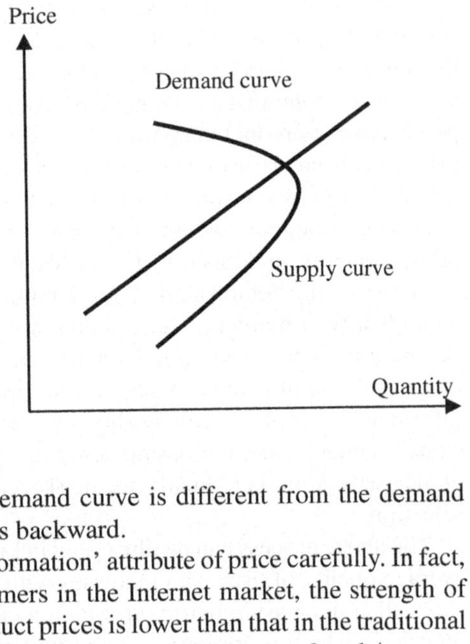

Fig. 2.3 Relationship between market price and demand of used cars

curve usually slopes upward, but the demand curve is different from the demand curve in traditional economics—it bends backward.

Therefore, we need to look at the 'information' attribute of price carefully. In fact, due to the 'lemon sensitivity' of consumers in the Internet market, the strength of quality signals reflected by Internet product prices is lower than that in the traditional market. The analysis of this problem will be carried out in Chapters 3 and 4.

2.2.2.3 The Complex Adaptability Embodied in the 'Lemon Market' Model

The adverse selection process embodied in the 'lemon market' model reflects the complex adaptability in the market operation: in fact, it is a process in which an

Adaptive Agent, including the buyers and sellers of used cars, changes their behavior and structure purposefully and directionally in the communication and interaction with the environment to achieve a reasonable state of adapting to the environment. For example, the average judgment of the buyer on the quality of the used car market is the way he behaves when entering the market. It is determined by the objectivity of human behavior.

In order to study the theory of complex adaptive system (CAS),[11] the Economic Science Laboratory of Renmin University of China established and verified the 'lemon market' model in 1999 by using Swarm, a modeling tool for CAS research provided by Santa Fe Research Institute.[12]

The objects involved in this model include:

1. Cars: Cars are the objects traded in the market. For the sake of simplicity, it is considered that there are only two kinds of cars in the automobile market, which are high quality and low quality, respectively, and their expected selling prices are 2000 yuan and 4000 yuan, respectively. Every car entering the market has the same possibility of being inquired. After an inquiry for a car, if the price given by the buyer is higher than the expected selling price, the transaction is successful, otherwise, the transaction is completed according to a given lower probability. This is consistent with the actual market situation, that is, the possibility of selling a car at a loss remains at a very low level. In fact, a car object in the model represents the sum of the car and its seller (the attributes of the car and the behavior of the seller).
2. Market: Market is another object involved in the model. Here the market is designed to have a fixed capacity. The market can record the current number of high-quality and low-quality cars, and also record the current number of high-quality and low-quality cars sold. Trading in the market is carried out round by round. In order to show the information asymmetry between the two parties in the market, for the seller, the information of the automobile is complete, that is, the seller knows whether the automobile is of high quality or low quality, but the buyer does not know whether the automobile is of high quality or low quality, so he can only predict the proportion of high-quality and low-quality automobiles in the market according to the previous transaction and give the expected price of the

---

[11] Complex Adaptive System (CAS) theory is a brand-new theory put forward by American scientist Holland (1994). This theory emphasizes that micro-subjects with 'adaptability' can interact with their surroundings and other subjects, and change their own structure and behavior through 'experience accumulation' (learning) in the process of interaction. The system composed of such subjects will develop in the interaction between subjects and environment and between subjects, showing the complex evolution process of macro system.

[12] Swarm software platform is a standard software toolset developed by Santa Fe Institute on the basis of complex adaptive system theory. This toolset can provide a very good software experimental environment. By building a computer model based on Swarm and calling the rich class library provided by the platform, we can conveniently simulate the research in many fields. The aim is to help scientists build a well-equipped software laboratory by providing them with a set of standard, flexible and reliable software tools. It runs on UNIX and Windows, and supports Java and Objective C. At the end of 1997, Professor Chen Yu of Renmin University of China visited Santa Fe Laboratory and began to introduce, publicize and popularize Swarm in China.

automobile purchased by the buyer on this basis. After a transaction takes place in the market, a new seller needs to enter the market. If a car cannot be sold after several rounds of transactions, it will automatically withdraw from the market. Considering the actual market situation, when a new seller enters the market, whether the sold vehicles are of high quality or low quality is also determined by the proportion of high and low-quality vehicles sold in the previous transaction.

Each of the above two objects has its own behavior. For the seller, each car in each transaction determines whether it is inquired according to a given probability. Once inquired, the expected price of the seller and the buyer is judged. If the buyer bids higher than the seller's price, the transaction will be completed; otherwise, the transaction will be decided according to a lower given transaction rate. The market's action after this round of trading is to count the respective quantities of high-quality and low-quality cars sold in this round of trading and calculate the buyer's expected price for the next round of trading according to this quantity. For cars that have completed the transaction and those that cannot be sold after multiple rounds of transactions, they will automatically withdraw from the market and be supplemented by new cars.

According to the above model, the corresponding Swarm model is established, and the actual operation shows that the simulation results are in good agreement with the prediction of the model. As shown in Fig. 2.4: The control panel controls the start, end and step-by-step operation of the model operation; the observer Cars market Observer sets its refresh frequency; Cars market Swarm sets the number of participating cars and the probability of being inquired; the Akerlof model shows that the change of the sum of all car sales prices over time is the main part. As can be seen in Fig. 2.4, the total price of all cars sold in the market is gradually decreasing, indicating that high-quality cars are gradually squeezed out of the market. It can be seen that the theoretical analysis is in good agreement with the experimental results.

The result of Swarm tells us that adverse selection in market transactions is actually determined by the objectivity of human behavior. In Akerlof model, buyers and sellers, as agents, have their own behavior rules. They relate and act with each other in

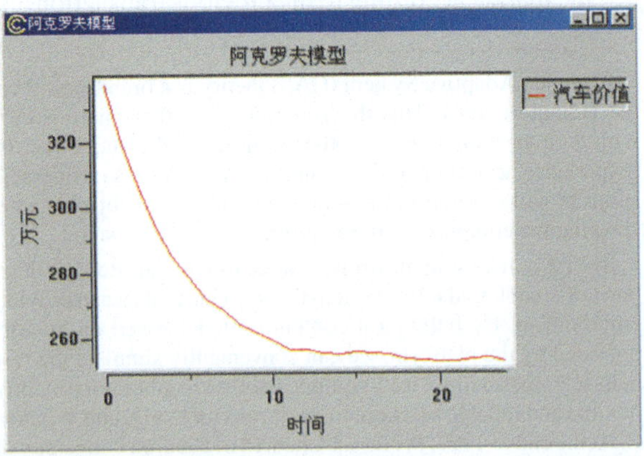

Fig. 2.4 Akerlof model in Swarm Running results on the platform

complex adaptive systems and finally produce a kind of 'equilibrium'. Although this result occurs in the traditional market, it is also true in the Internet market—because the objectivity of human behavior has not changed.

2.2.2.4 Adverse Selection Conditions and Changes in Market Competition Forms

In the traditional perfect competition theory, all products in the market are assumed to have the same quality. Therefore, a manufacturer who can sell products at a lower price (constant quality) must mean an increase in production efficiency, and it can produce products of the same quality at a lower cost. In market competition, price competition can often defeat opponents and win the market. However, when the information of 'quality' can be hidden, its premise and conclusion will change.

Therefore, the 'lemon' principle tells us that the most important form of market competition in asymmetric market formed under the condition of asymmetric information is non-price competition. Therefore, in order to change consumers' judgment of quality by price and make consumers think that its low-priced products are of high quality, enterprises selling low-priced products must convince consumers that their products are of high quality through some non-price activities of competition, so as to distinguish them from 'lemon' products. This point is particularly important for the Internet market. In fact, a large part of this study is to discuss and analyze this problem and we will carry out the specific content in the following chapters.

2.3 Literature Review: The Evolution Track and Enlightenment of 'Lemon Market' Model

Adverse selection theory has established its position in economics because of its extensive and far-reaching influence. In the adverse selection theory, 'lemon market' model is of great significance, which provides a basic analytical framework and theoretical basis for the establishment of this theory. Since Akerlof put forward this model, many economists have expanded and extended this model along with the work initiated by Professor Akerlof and obtained abundant research results.

Now, we analyze and summarize the evolution track of 'lemon market' model in the past 30 years and discuss the influence of 'lemon market' model on this study and the possible development direction in the future, in order to lay a foundation for us to analyze Internet adverse selection and establish Internet 'lemon market' model.

2.3.1 *The Evolution Track of the 'Lemon Market' Model*

2.3.1.1 The Ranking of Pareto Efficiency Standards and the Essence of Market Equilibrium

The expansion and deepening of the 'lemon market' model is first manifested in the reset of the premise assumptions in the model. Wilson [26], a professor of economics at Wisconsin University in the United States, improved Akerlof's 'lemon market' model (referred to as Akerlof model for short). Wilson's point of view is that when buyers' preferences are inconsistent, there are many kinds of Walrasian equilibrium, which can be graded by Pareto efficiency criteria. He pointed out that if the premise assumption in the model is relaxed to the existence of differences in consumption preferences and uneven quality distribution among buyers, it can be concluded that:

1. Different from the conclusion of single equilibrium solution in Akerlof model, there may be Multiple-Walrasian Equilibrium in Wilson model, that is to say, there may be multiple equilibrium points with equal supply and demand. Because the average quality level of used cars is not a constant in Wilson's model, the increase of price level in a certain range may cause a larger number of used cars to join the supply, which leads to the increase of average quality and actual demand of used cars entering the transaction with the increase of price. If the demand curve contains a part sloping to the upper right, it will have more than one focus with the supply curve, so we can get multiple Walras equilibrium solutions or multiple Pareto optimal solutions.
2. There is a Pareto ordering in this Multiple-Walrasian Equilibrium, in which the higher-price equilibrium is superior to the low-price equilibrium. Wilson's analysis shows that although sellers always want to sell cars with a given quality level at the highest possible price to obtain more profits, buyers are also willing to obtain an equilibrium result with a higher price, because the increase in average quality level caused by the increase in price is enough to make up for the utility loss caused by the increase in price. In this way, when both buyers and sellers tend to the Walrasian Equilibrium with high prices, the welfare level of all people improves. Wilson argues that if buyers have a fixed marginal substitution rate between the quality of the car and the consumption of other goods, each buyer will prefer a higher equilibrium price to a lower equilibrium price. In this way, there is a sort of Pareto Criterion.

In order to further explain the market structure under the condition of adverse selection, Wilson [27] further analyzed the essence of market equilibrium in the market with adverse selection. By extending the Akerlof model, the author analyzes the market equilibrium in three cases: (1) the auctioneer's bid; (2) Buyer's bid; (3) Seller's bid. Through analysis, he believes that only when the auctioneer bids will there be a single price equilibrium. Whether the buyer or the seller bids, the price distribution is accompanied by the existence of excessive supply. Therefore, the author thinks that in the market with serious adverse selection, the way of commodity allocation is very sensitive to the means of bidding. Both buyers and sellers may prefer to trade in a market that leads to perpetual oversupply, rather than choose a price level that can make the market reach an equilibrium between supply and demand.[13]

After that, Rose [23] of the University of Sydney, Australia, deduced and verified the Walrasian Equilibrium described in Wilson model with strict mathematical methods. He assumes that the quality of used cars is five common generalized distributions (Gamma distribution, Chi-squared distribution, Exponential distribution, Lognormal distribution and Normal distribution) and obtains their demand curves. His conclusion is that the first four quality distributions do not exist because their demand curves are inclined downward to the right, but when the quality distribution is Normal distribution (Normal distribution) and the price level is low, the demand curve may be inclined upward and then Multiple-Walrasian Equilibrium points may appear.

In addition, Kim [18] of the State University of New York analyzed the Walrasian paradigm described by Akerlof [1] and Wilson [27] in a market with severe information asymmetry from two aspects. First, he argues that while Akerlof correctly points to possible market failures in the used car market, his analysis ignores the possibility that market participants are free to switch roles. Secondly, the author's model is based on the quality of used cars as an endogenous variable, which is different from Wilson's model. In this paper, the author analyzes two different situations: in the first case, given the new car price and the type of market participants, there is a unique equilibrium point; the second case is similar to the Akerlof–Wilson model, where not only the 'lemon' principle may occur but also the multiple Walras equilibria in the Wilson model. However, in this case, if market participants have the ability to change their roles at no cost, it will make it impossible to rank the Pareto criterion.

2.3.1.2 Game Analysis and Offset System

Heal [11], a professor of economics at Sussex University in England analyzed the Akerlof model and its conclusions with game theory as a tool. He divided the marketing strategies adopted by each product seller into two types: 'high' quality and 'low' quality. Through analysis, he found that as long as the game played by market participants is not a game but an infinite number of repeated games, there may be a cooperative Nash equilibrium. His conclusion is that only when the seller is extremely short-sighted, that is to say, only pays attention to the current interests, will there be a phenomenon of 'defective products driving out good products', otherwise market participants are willing to trade with high-quality products. Professor Akerlof [2, 3] answered Heal's question. He pointed out that although the market participants will have the cooperative game in order to avoid the market failure caused by the 'lemon' problem, the occurrence of this game must be guaranteed by the corresponding system, and its function is to link the past, present and future together, so that this game behavior will happen and repeat constantly.

[13] This view was explained by Stiglitz and Weiss [24] about credit rationing [24].

In fact, the above debate further proves the role of 'counteracting institutions' proposed by Professor Akerlof in that classic paper. As Professor Akerlof pointed out in his paper, many market mechanisms actually appear to solve the problem of asymmetric information, because economic agents have strong motivation to offset adverse selection related to market efficiency. For example, providing guarantees in transactions, making consumers agree by building brands, establishing reputation by setting up chain stores and providing certified service records have played this role. Professor Heal said that the game needs the guarantee of this system to go on. The argument between Professor Heal and Professor Akerlof illustrates the role of institutions in solving adverse selection.

Recently, there are still some economists who focus their research on the 'lemon' problem on institutional analysis. For example, Hendel and Lizzeri [12, 13] of Princeton University in the United States emphasized the role of non-market institutions in solving asymmetric information problems in the process of dynamic analysis of 'lemon market' model, including certification intermediary and lease contract.

2.3.1.3 Experimental Research

As an effective analytical method, experimental economics has unique charm and persuasiveness in the analysis of economic phenomena. Some economists use experimental methods to deepen and expand the Akerlof model.

Bond [6], an economics professor at the State University of New York, published a paper *Direct Test of Lemon Market Model: Second-hand convertible truck market* in *American Economic Review*. Through experiments, the author concluded that if the maintenance time or life of a car can be controlled, there is no difference between an old car and a new car. The author thinks that there are two possible explanations for this phenomenon: the first one is that the offset system mentioned by Professor Akerlof is working and being developed; the second explanation is that buyers can obtain enough information through searching to reduce the asymmetry of information. But the market is still inefficient if reducing information asymmetry, such as through offset systems or through search, requires high costs. Therefore, Professor Bond's experimental research on Akerlof model shows that the influence of used cars and new cars on the market lies not in the 'new' and 'old' cars, but in the role of offset system, as well as the efficiency and cost of search.

In recent years, economists' experiments on the 'lemon' problem are more concentrated on the study of some unique individual markets. For example, Chezum and Wimmer (1997) of St. Lawrence University in the United States conducted an experimental study on adverse selection in the auction market of one-year-old stallions. They used data from the Keeneland stallion auction market. In this market, sellers are divided into two categories: those who sell only part of their own stallions as horse racers, and those who sell all their stallions as specialized breeders. Obviously, the first type of seller is more motivated to train his stallion than the second type. If buyers can't confirm the type of seller, they can only expect less from the quality of stallions, which leads to lower prices for the first type of sellers.

Couton et al. [8] made an empirical study on the French automobile market from 1991 to 1992 by using Hedonic Price model. The results show that the environmental and safety characteristics of the market and the delay on consumers will have a real impact on consumers' behavior. By analyzing the relationship between perceived quality and price in some markets, he proved that there is Akerlof effect in French automobile market, which cannot be explained by inflation.

In addition, Hotl [14], an economics professor at the University of Virginia in the United States, will also bring 'lemon' into classroom experiments. In the experiment, students were divided into two groups of 'quality-price' grades. Experiments show that under the condition of complete information, the market price and grade can quickly reach the most efficient level, and everyone can get the maximum surplus; but if only the price, not the grade, is known to the purchaser, the grade and price are reduced to the suboptimal efficiency level. The authors point out that such experimental results could stimulate discussion on topics such as asymmetric information market failures and remedial measures such as quality standards and guarantees.

2.3.2 The Latest Research Progress of 'Lemon Market' Model

2.3.2.1 The Dynamic 'Lemon Market' Model

Hendel and Lizzeri [12] found that the second-hand market in the United States has never disappeared, on the contrary, the transaction volume is still very large, and the market distortion is lower than previously thought. On the assumption that reputation deteriorates with the decline of quality, there are still a large number of transactions occurring with the price decline. In order to explain this phenomenon, they constructed a dynamic adverse selection model and emphasized that the main difference between the model constructed by themselves and the standard adverse selection model is that it can reveal the interactive relationship between the new product market and the resale market more clearly. The model shows that in the case of adverse selection, the price of a new car is higher than that when it is not in the market. By comparing several different brands of cars, they found that cars with unreliable brands have greater price declines and lower market transactions. Finally, they came to the conclusion that the natural depreciation of automobiles is more important than adverse selection.

Janssen and Karamychev [16] of Erasmus University in Rotterdam, Netherlands, further explored the nature of market failure in dynamic Akerlof model. In the Akerlof model of durable goods market constructed by them, the market equilibrium in this model shows the characteristics of Cycles and Multiple Equilibrium. One of their main conclusions is that in the equilibrium of dynamic model, sellers with high-quality products wait longer than sellers with low-quality products; for any quality distribution, there must be an infinite number of multiple cycle equilibria, when all products can be traded at a specific time after they enter the market.

2.3.2.2 The Seller's Information Structure and Market Welfare

Kessler [17], University of Bonn, Germany, explores how market performance depends on the seller's information structure in a market with adverse selection. She extended the standard adverse selection competition model in her paper 'Looking at the Lemon Market Again', and he allowed market participants with information side to have different Information Structures related to quality. He believes that the analytical framework used by Akerlof in his classic paper is a stylized market analysis framework, and the situation shown by Akerlof will disappear only when the seller knows the quality of the car and obtains a small profit from the transaction. It actually implies the fact that one side of the market is ignorant and the other side's information structure is perfect, however, in many cases this situation is very vague. By introducing welfare factors into the analytical model, the author tests the welfare characteristics under the condition of market equilibrium and draws a conclusion that this equilibrium is obtained on the premise that sellers have less information than their own transactions. Finally, the author points out that the increase of market performance of sellers with less information depends on their potential profits in market transactions and the average characteristics of sellers' information structure.

What is more challenging is that Professor Levin [20] of Stanford University has made a bolder reflection on the Akerlof model, and he thinks that greater information asymmetry may not necessarily reduce the income in transactions. Firstly, the author observes the relationship between information asymmetry and transaction and points out that there are two competitive results: for a fixed supply curve, when the seller has more information, the demand curve will move down and the 'Buyer's Curse' will be stronger; however, a fall in demand in turn leads to a fall in supply, and the supply curve also shifts downward. In this way, the information will classify sellers: on the one hand, it will drive some sellers out of the market, on the other hand, it will also send some sellers back to the market. The author points out that for the segmented information structure, we can get a very extreme result: when new information appears in the market, the seller may be driven out of the market and the transaction will decline; if new information is popular in the market, the market price will remain unchanged and the transaction will not be affected; if exiting vendors get new information, transactions may increase as long as vendors with bad news are pushed back to the market; if the maximum transaction cannot be obtained under the given information structure, the maximum transaction cannot be obtained even if the seller's information is improved. Based on the work done by Lenmann [19] and Athey and Levin [5] in decision theory, the author establishes his own model and verifies the above observation results through the model. Therefore, the author concludes that the increase of transactions depends on the relative amount of these influences. Levin used the model to analyze the change of transaction volume if the seller's information is released to the buyer. The author believes that public information can create new markets because market prices depend on public signals.

Although the expectation of equilibrium trading will increase or decrease, we can still get positive results if the market works well. Therefore, the author argues that increasing the information of buyers, that is, the socialization of private information, will definitely promote the growth of transactions—as long as the market demand curve slopes downward.

2.3.2.3 The 'Lemon Market' on the Internet

Today, the Internet economy is getting better and better, and the 'lemon' problem in the Internet market has also attracted the attention of some economists. Huston and Spence [15] of Trinity University in the United States think that although the Internet makes consumers buy goods across the space distance, there is still information asymmetry because consumers can't check the quality of goods. The author builds a model and tests his hypothesis based on the data obtained from the coinage auction market on the Internet. The results show that only 87 cents per dollar of the coins sold for which the price increases with the quality is considered to increase with the quality, which shows that consumers underestimate the seller's commitment to the increase in quality. The experimental data also show that the information asymmetry of the unidentified coinage is greater than that of the identified coinage, so the unidentified coinage has a more serious 'lemon' problem. Choi et al. [7], an economist at the University of Texas in the United States, wrote 'The Economics of Electronic Commerce'. The book mainly tells the economic reasons why the Internet market can't work without product information. Although the book does not explain to us the theoretical roots of the failure of the Internet market, it reveals a very important point: Although virtual transactions provide a good way to reduce transaction costs, its future development will mainly depend on the solutions to economic problems rather than technical problems.

2.3.3 Conclusion and Enlightenment

Looking at Akerlof's classical theory and its evolution, we can find that economists have expanded and deepened this model in the past 30 years. At the same time, it brings the following enlightenment for us to study the Internet 'lemon' problem and establish the 'lemon market' model in the Internet market:

2.3.3.1 The Continuation and Refinement of the Research Content

According to the order of time, we can express the emphasis that economists pay attention to as follows: adverse selection → offset system → Walrasian Equilibrium (the order of Pareto Efficiency standard) → the essence of market equilibrium → experimental research → seller's information structure → 'lemon market' model on the Internet. By extending, refining and modifying the classical Akerlof model, economists make it more explanatory and convincing to the real market.

Therefore, in the Internet market, it is still our focus to study the Walras equilibrium, the essence of market equilibrium and non-market system under the condition of adverse selection. At the same time, we should pay more attention to the refinement of market and the refinement of market information structure.

2.3.3.2 The Exploration of Research Methods

It is an important supplement and extension to the theoretical analysis to study the 'lemon market' model with the methods of experimental economics and dynamic methods. In fact, besides the economists listed in this paper, there are also some experimental economists who use computer simulation technology and complex adaptation theory (CAS) to analyze and study the 'lemon market' model and have achieved certain results [28].

In fact, due to the multi-faceted nature of Internet space, we also need to communicate, complement and synthesize among disciplines when studying the Internet 'lemon' problem. At present, there are relatively few such studies.

2.3.3.3 The Future Research Direction

The future research on Akerlof model may or should be carried out in three aspects: the research object may be expanded from physical market to Internet market; the research content will pay more attention to the influence of the change of market information structure on transaction equilibrium; in the research methods, more static analysis will be changed to dynamic analysis, more experimental economics methods will be adopted, more attention will be paid to the study of typical markets and more computer simulation methods will be adopted.

We are gratified that the 'lemon' problem in the Internet market has attracted the attention of some economists. Although the analysis of the 'lemon' problem in the Internet market is still at a relatively primary stage, the unique expression of the 'lemon' problem in the Internet market will surely attract more economists' attention and draw more valuable conclusions. This paper tries to contribute to this.

References

1. Akerlof GA (1970) The market for 'lemon': qualitative uncertainty and the market mechanism. Quart J Econ 84(3):488–500
2. Akerlof GA (1976) Reply to professor hear. Quart J Econ 90(3):503

3. Akerlof GA (1976) The economics of caste and of the rat race and other woeful tales. Quart J Econ 90(4):599–617
4. Akerlof GA (2001) Writing the "The market for 'lemons'": a personal and interpretive essay. http://www.nobel.se/economics/articles/akerlof/index.html
5. Athey S, Levin J (1998) The value of information in monotone decision problems. Working Paper No. 98, Department of Economics, MIT
6. Bond EW (1982) A direct test of the 'lemons' model: the market for used pickup trucks. Am Econ Rev 72:836–840
7. Chezum B, Wimmer B (1997) Roses or lemons: Adverse selection in the market for thoroughbred yearlings, Review of E-conomics & Statistics 79:521–526.
8. Choi SY, Stahl DO, Whinston AB (1997) The economics of electronic commerce. Macmillan Technical Publishing, Indianapolis
9. Couton C, Gardes F, Thepaut Y (1996) Hedonic prices for environment and safety characteristic and Akerlof effect in the French car market. Appl Econ Lett 3:435–440
10. Dodds WB, Monroe KB, Grewal D (1991) Effects of price. South Econ J 64:628–647
11. Eatwell J, Milgate M, Newman P (1987) The new Palgrave dictionary of economics. The Macmillan Press.
12. Heal G (1976) Do bad products drive out good? Quart J Econ 90(3):499–502
13. Hendel I, Lizzeri A (1999) Adverse selection in durable goods. Markets Am Econ Rev 89(5):1097–1115
14. Hendel I, Lizzeri A (2002) The role of leasing under adverse selection. J Polit Econ 110:113–143
15. Holland, JL (1994) The Self-Directed Search. Odessa, FL: Psychological Assessment Resources
16. Hotl A (1999) Charles and Roger Sherman. Classroom games: a market for lemons. J Econ Perspect 13:205–214
17. Huston JH, Spence RW (2002) Quality, uncertainty and the internet: the market for cyber lemon. Am Econ 46(1):50–60
18. Janssen MCW, Karamychev VA (2002) Cycles and multiple equilibria in the market for durable lemons. Econ Theor 20:579–601
19. Johnson WR (1985) The economics of copying, Political Econom 93:158–174.
20. Kessler AS (2001) Revisiting the lemons market. Int Econ Rev 42(1):25–41
21. Kim J-C (1985) The market for 'lemons' reconsidered: a model of the used car market with asymmetric information. Am Econ Rev 75(4):836–843
22. Lenmann EL (1988) Comparing location experiments. Ann Stat 16:521–533
23. Levin J (2001) Information and the market for lemons. RAND J Econ 32:657–666
24. Olshavsky RW, Aylesworth AB, Kempf DS (1995) The price-choice relationship: a contingent processing approach. J Bus Res 33:207–218
25. Rasmusen E (1994) Game and information, 2rd edn. Blackwell Publishers.
26. Rose C (1993) Equilibrium and adverse selection. Rand J Econ 24:559–569
27. Stiglitz J, Weiss A (1981) Credit rationing in markets with imperfect information. Am Econ Rev 71(3):393–410
28. Teas RK, Agarwal S (2000) The effect of extrinsic product cues on consumers' perceptions of quality, sacrifice, and value. J Acad Mark Sci 28(2):278–290
29. Wilson C (1979) Equilibrium and adverse selection. Am Econ Rev 69(2):313–317
30. Wilson C (1980) The nature of equilibrium in markets with adverse selection. Bell J Econ 11:108–130
31. Yu C (2000) Systems science (Chapter 8). Shanghai Science and Technology Education Press, Shanghai

Chapter 3
Adverse Selection of Internet Market: Mathematical Model and Theoretical Explanation

The purpose of this chapter is to provide a basic point of theoretical analysis for the following chapters. In this chapter, we first analyze the causes of adverse selection in the Internet market, and describe the Internet 'lemon' problem in fact. Then, on this basis, we build a mathematical model of Internet adverse selection and verify it. As a generalization and extension of the theoretical model, this chapter will also analyze the relationship between Internet market and physical market under adverse selection. Finally, according to the conclusions provided by the theoretical model, the theoretical ideas to solve the Internet adverse selection are put forward.

3.1 The Formation and Performance of Adverse Selection in the Internet Market

3.1.1 The Characteristics of Internet Products and Transactions

3.1.1.1 The Definition of Internet Products

Product is a collection of benefits in essence from economics. It satisfies the desire of an organization or consumer to exchange it for money or something of other value. With the development of Internet, the basic characteristics of products in e-commerce market will also change. Although selling physical products on the Internet is the primary goal of many Internet stores, their core goal is to increase the efficiency of

Y. Pan, *Trust Management in the Chinese E-Commerce Market*,
Advanced Studies in E-Commerce, https://doi.org/10.1007/978-981-97-1115-4_3

business transactions or improve services and expand market share. Their creative ideas can transform many physical products and processes into digital products.[1]

Information is the preferred example of digital products. Information products include a wide range of paper products, such as books, magazines, newspapers, periodicals, photos, maps and other graphics. Most of these products are first made into digital forms and then printed on paper. Some information products, such as databases and computer software, are disseminated and used in digital form. Audio-visual products can be digitized, so multimedia products such as movies, TV programs and sound products can be mixed with information products or sold separately as entertainment products. In addition, anything sent and received on the Internet can become a digital product. All kinds of paper products can be turned into digital products by scanning or by changing the way we use them. For example, air tickets, concert tickets or baseball tickets don't need to be printed on paper, they can be digitized, transmitted and stored in personal ID cards. You can also log on to a website to make reservations and pay digitally. Tickets can also be downloaded to customers' storage devices, and only need to be scanned when boarding.

Although some products or services have no corresponding physical form, they can become digital products as long as they exist in the form of knowledge or process. For example, the knowledge and experience of a salesperson or doctor can be digitized, made into a document or program, and then sold to customers. Similarly, the process of human interaction and communication can be integrated into a digital process or an electronic market. For example, the auction of products can form an electronic auction market, where items to be auctioned can be browsed Internet and bidding and payment can be made electronically.

3.1.1.2 Characteristics of Internet Product Transactions

Internet product is a special kind of product. In many cases, it is virtual and does not need physical existence. At the same time, it can spread in many ways. We should regard it as a consumable product to analyze its economic connotation.

1. Subjectivity of Internet product utility evaluation

The demand for any product changes with the inherent taste difference of consumers, while the demand for information products seems to change more easily. Because information and other products have no physical form, it brings up the subjectivity of consumers' evaluation of their utility. Therefore, sellers of information products should rely more on consumer information in order to classify consumers according to their preferences. In addition, product customization and differential pricing based on consumers' types or other identity information in Internet marketing are relatively different in use and value, so the evaluation of its utility is subjective.

[1] Although many of the products discussed in this study are physical products, in the Internet market, it must first be represented in the form of digital products, that is, in the form of virtual products. Therefore, when discussing Internet products, we should first consider its digital characteristics.

2. Short-term and cumulative utility of Internet products

We often say that 'outdated information is not information', because the value of many information products depends on time. For example, weather information is used to forecast crop yields, and yesterday's weather information is no longer useful unless it is used for archiving and reference. But short-term information has its own value for archiving and reference. This value lies in the accumulation effect. A part of any information file can be recycled to produce different products. Not only consumption but also the production of information is an accumulative and usually cooperative process. In the process of spreading through accumulation, modification, addition and improvement, information is often evolved and modified.

3. Extensity of Internet products

In economics, extensity refers to the economic consequences that cannot be completely explained by price principle and market theory, which may be unexpected gains or unexpected losses in advance. For example, although cars pollute the air, the increased cost of polluting the environment is not reflected in the price of cars, which is a negative extensity. If your neighbor's trees give you shade, this is a positive extensity. Many products have Internet externals. That is to say, if more people use a product, its value will increase.

Internet extensity can be manifested as both positive externality and negative extensity. Internet extensity can be obtained directly by increasing the number of users. For example, the telephone is of low value if no one uses it, but it is of much greater value if everyone uses it. Congestion is a negative extensity that counteracts positive Internet extensity. If everyone uses the phone, you will benefit, while if they keep calling so that you can't get in, you will be upset that the line is always busy. Another example of Internet extensity is the software industry. More companies will develop applications for users who use popular operating systems, such as Windows, rather than non-popular operating systems.

4. Variability and differentiation of Internet product content

The content of digital products is changeable at any time, and they can be easily customized or modified at any time. Such modifications—whether unintentional, intentional or fraudulent—are inevitable. Therefore, due to the nature of digital products, manufacturers cannot control the integrity of their products. Although free documents on the Internet only allow the spread of unmodified copies, in the world of 0 and 1, this rule is practically unenforceable. Still, manufacturers are using a variety of methods to deal with such modifications, such as techniques to prevent random modifications, such as PDF files that can be read by Adobe's Acrobat Reader, but users cannot store files in digital form.

The variability of Internet products makes the production of Internet producers not to protect the integrity of content, but to differentiate their products, for example, upgrade their products and sell them as interactive services instead of standard shrink-packaged products. Product differentiation is not only possible, but also the business strategy of digital product companies.

5. The priori nature of Internet products

To establish the consumption preference of digital products, consumers must use them in advance, and then they can compare their utilities and make choices.

6. Physical characteristics of Internet products

Digital products can't be worn out. Once they are created, they can exist forever. No matter how long or how often it is used, the quality of digital products will not decline, which is very different from ordinary material products.

Above, we analyzed the characteristics of Internet market products, which are different from traditional markets. In fact, it is these characteristics different from the physical market and the virtuality of Internet trade that determine the 'lemon' problem in the Internet market, which will also have characteristics different from the traditional market. This is what we will discuss next.

3.1.2 The Asymmetry of Information in the Internet Market and the Internet 'Lemon' Problem

Compared with the traditional market, the advantages of e-commerce market lie in its lower barriers to entry, lower management costs and easy access to market information. The reason why it has lower barriers to entry is that the Internet provides equal opportunities for all market participants, where large companies have no inherent advantages over small companies. In the physical market, big is a very effective market signal, but in the e-commerce market, big and product quality are not necessarily related, which reduces the barriers to market entry. Another characteristic of e-commerce market is that it can search comprehensively and obtain information at low cost or no cost. Because automatic search and classification technology solve this problem, you can search for information in large quantities and effectively with the help of search services. Therefore, compared with the traditional market, it has more ways to obtain market information, higher efficiency and lower cost, which means that the completeness of information acquisition is higher. At the same time, because this kind of information search on the Internet is low cost and no cost, it also means relatively low transaction costs.

Although e-commerce market has such advantages, especially its high information efficiency, it does not mean that it has high market efficiency. In fact, compared with the traditional market, the adverse selection problem caused by the asymmetry of product quality information in e-commerce market not only exists, but also is more serious. The main reasons are:

3.1.2.1 The Subjectivity of Internet Product Utility Evaluation and the Subjectivity of Product Quality Evaluation Caused by the Externality of the Internet

Because digital products are not only the digital version of paper products, but also contain the characteristics of electronic media, for example, Internet newspapers are personalized and customized, and can be updated at any time, so the quality evaluation will become more subjective and personalized, and it will be more uncertain. However, the negative externality of the Internet makes it difficult for the reputation established by suppliers in one consumer to spread to other consumers, which further aggravates the existence of information asymmetry.

3.1.2.2 The Information Asymmetry Caused by the Physical Characteristics of Internet Products

This mainly refers to the problems caused by the non-destructiveness of digital products. In the Internet market, a large part of products are digital products. Because digital products do not appear tangible wear like other material products, that is, they are non-destructive, so digital products can exist forever once they are created. Although the initial product quality of digital products will become obvious because of consumers' use behavior, no matter how long or how frequently they are used, the quality of digital products will not decline, that is to say, there is no difference between durable and non-durable digital products, and there is no difference between products sold from manufacturers and second-hand goods. It is precisely because of this situation that the manufacturers of digital products are competing with the products they have sold. Because most consumers can only buy the same competitive product once, the manufacturer adopts a deliberately outdated and frequently upgraded sales strategy, even if there are no competitors. For example, although some software has been upgraded for many years, it actually contains some useless functions that customers can't use, which in turn wastes customers' learning time. Therefore, in the Internet market, the quality information that the price of Internet products can transmit is very limited. As it is not known whether the quality of many new versions is higher than that of the old versions, the 'lemon' problem caused by the quality uncertainty will become more prominent.

3.1.2.3 The Variability and Differentiation of Internet Product Content, and the Information Asymmetry Caused by the Difficulty of Identifying the Identity of Internet Traders

In the electronic marketplace, it is difficult to identify sellers: an Internet store can be set up in one day or disappear the next. Because of this uncertainty, the efficiency of market operation will be very low, or even unable to operate at all. In addition, the identity of Internet traders is not easy to identify, which also leads to the existence of the Internet 'lemon' problem. For example, although Internet auction has become an important market transaction mechanism on the Internet, which can effectively improve transaction efficiency and reduce transaction costs, there is a serious problem of information asymmetry between the two parties in the Internet auction market. The specific performance is as follows: because the auctioneer and the bidding bidder do not know each other before the auction, they do not meet each other during the auction, and the probability of meeting after the auction is almost zero; in addition, all the traders participating in the Internet auction appear in the auction website as virtual identities (ID), which makes even the auction website unable to know the true identity of the registered users in detail. If the Internet users change their ID, others cannot carefully identify whether the new ID and the original old ID belong to the same person.[2]

Furthermore, the information provided by suppliers pursues a differentiated strategy—it prevents the possibility of comparing bids. Therefore, some information cannot or will not become comparable and verifiable information. In addition, the short-term utility of Internet products leads to the frequent evolution of information, which also aggravates the information disadvantage of consumers.

3.1.2.4 The Quality of Internet Products Is Not Easy to Check Due to the Priori Nature

Because digital products are mostly Experience Goods, their quality can only be understood after use. However, once consumers master the information content of digital products, consumers are no longer willing to buy them—this is the insurmountable 'Information Paradox' [2] in the production of information products. This characteristic makes manufacturers have no good way to convince consumers of the quality of their products. At the same time, because the quality of experienced products can only be known through experience and actual use by consumers, consumers will not buy them even if a large number of advertisements and product information are not enough to convince consumers of their quality. Customers may take a risk if they know that quality is beneficial to future purchases, but if they only use a product once, the risk is very small.

The transcendental nature of Internet products requires marketers to reduce the uncertainty and asymmetry of product quality information through various marketing means to help consumers understand the utility of new products, so that consumers can establish their own purchase preferences. For example, when MS-DOS and Windows operating system entered the Chinese market, they achieved the goal of

[2] The process of Internet auction transactions is as follows: Almost all auction websites require traders (auctioneers and bidders) to register a user name (ID) before the first transaction, and then list the auction items and relevant information of auctioneers. Bidders choose their intended auction items and participate in bidding. After winning the auction items, the bidder with the highest bidding price pays the auctioneer shopping funds at the auction price. After receiving the purchase money, the auctioneer delivers the auction items (because the two parties do not know each other in the auction, mailing becomes the most important way to deliver the items).

popularization through low price, free installation and gift, and even turned a blind eye to piracy. However, in the late 1990s, after Windows operating system was basically popularized in China, it raised its retail price in China, even higher than the domestic price in the United States, and intensified its efforts to crack down on piracy, which once caused tension between Microsoft and domestic computer vendors. This kind of practice or marketing strategy of Microsoft Corporation is to make use of the transcendental nature of digital products, so that consumers have path dependence on their products and increase the transfer cost of consumers. Although we cannot evaluate the advantages and disadvantages of Microsoft’s practice, its effect is obviously locked-in to consumers who are at an information disadvantage.

3.1.2.5 Information Asymmetry Caused by the Diversity of Internet Producers

Different from physical products, digital products are manufactured and sold by virtual people on the Internet, and the sales time of market sellers is short and the number is large. Every user is a producer and a potential seller through today’s personal homepage and a Web server that may run on any personal computer in the future. Therefore, in this case, the asymmetry of quality information of Internet products will be greater, and adverse selection will be more serious.

3.2 The Construction of the Internet ‘Lemon Market’ Model

In the previous chapter, we made a qualitative analysis and description of the Internet ‘lemon’. Now, we will establish an adverse selection model (‘lemon market’ model) in Internet trade to discuss the market operation mechanism under the condition of asymmetric and uncertain quality information, so as to provide a theoretical basis and theoretical explanation for the Internet ‘lemon’ phenomenon and draw a conclusion.

3.2.1 The Premise of Establishing the Model: The Improvement of the Classic ‘Lemon Market’ Model

According to our previous analysis, the ‘lemon market’ model in the Internet market should have two outstanding characteristics:

Firstly, in the classical Akerlof model, the conditions of demand occurrence derived from utility function are all based on the relationship between average quality μ and price p. However, due to the virtual nature of Internet trade, it makes it more difficult for consumers to judge the average quality of Internet products through the probability distribution of product quality than traditional markets. Such a feature will lead consumers to make up for their lack of quality judgment by reducing their preference for the quality of Internet products [10].

Secondly, in the Akerlof model, all sellers actually imply the assumption that they are considered to have the same quality preference. However, in Internet trade, due to the virtuality and convenience of the Internet and the need of a certain marketing strategy (such as 'price discrimination'), the seller's evaluation of product quality may be different for different sales groups of the same product, that is to say, the evaluation of quality will be more subjective. This is a characteristic that we must show in the process of building a model, which is different from the physical market. Although economists after Akerlof extended the 'lemon market' model, these extensions are still aimed at the traditional physical market, and the premise in the model is only relaxed to the difference of consumers' preference for quality among buyers. Based on the virtual nature of the Internet, this model relaxes the presupposition of this model to the difference of product quality preference between buyers and between buyers and sellers.

3.2.2 The Basic Theoretical Model

Now, let's construct an Akerlof model or 'lemon' model for Internet trade. In the process of building the model, we mainly refer to some tools and conclusions of Molho [12] and Wilson [18, 19] when analyzing and expanding Akerlof model, and at the same time, according to the previous discussion, we add further stipulation on the behavior characteristics of buyers and sellers in Internet trade. We use Von Neumann-Morgenstern expected utility function and consider the influence of continuous quality distribution of Internet products on market equilibrium.

We divide the Internet market into two parts: buyer and seller, and denote the quality of Internet products by $q \in [q0, q1]$, and its quality distribution function is $f(q)$.

We will discuss it in the following parts:

3.2.2.1 The Seller

For Internet sellers (that is, potential sellers), his utility function is:

$$U_s = U_s(c, n|m, q) = c + mqn$$

Here c is the seller's consumption of other items; n is a discrete binary variable, which indicates whether the seller sells the product, $n = 1$ means not selling the product, and $n = 0$ means selling the product. m is a utility index, which reflects the vendor's evaluation of the quality of Internet products.[3] Because it is the absolute price, not the relative price, that affects the decision, we can define the price of the product as p and the price of other goods as 1.

The problems faced by sellers under the constraint of revenue budget are:

$$max_{c,n} U_S = c + mqn$$

Assume that its budget constraints are:

$$Y_S = c + pn$$

Here Y_S is the seller's income. When we substitute the budget constraint into the utility function, there are:

$$U_S = Y_S + (mq - p)n$$

If we want to maximize the utility of the seller when selling the product (that is, when $n = 0$), that is, the owner sells the product if and only if:

$$mq - p < 0, \text{ that is, } mq < p \text{ or } q < \frac{p}{m} \tag{3.1}$$

Then, at any price, the condition $q <$ the proportion of products is met: $\frac{p}{m}$

$$S(P) = prob\left(q < \frac{p}{m}\right) = \begin{cases} \int_{q^0}^{p/m} f(q)dq & (q > mq^0) \\ 0 & otherwise \end{cases} \tag{3.2}$$

3.2.2.2 The Buyer

For Internet consumers (that is, potential buyers), we assume that their utility function is:

$$U_B = U_B(c, r|t, q) = c + tqr$$

Here c is the buyer's consumption of other items; r is a variable that indicates whether the seller buys the product, $r = 1$ means to buy, and $r = 0$ means not to buy; t represents the relative evaluation parameter of Internet product quality compared with other goods consumption.[4] In order to ensure the smooth progress of transactions, t

[3] In fact, the [1] model implies the assumption that all vendors are actually considered to have the same quality preference, representing m as $m = 1$.

[4] Corresponding to Akerlof model, $t = 3/2$.

should be $\geq m$. We also use p to represent the price of products, while the price of other goods is defined as 1.

The problems faced by buyers under the constraint of revenue budget are:

$$max_{c,r} U_B = c + tqr$$

Assume that its budget constraints are:

$$Y_B = c + qr$$

Here Y_B is the buyer's income.

Like the basic assumption of Akerlof's [1] model, since consumers do not know the actual quality of each product, but can determine the average quality of products by means of speculation and estimation, especially in the Internet market because of the existence of virtuality, we now assume that the average quality level of products in the Internet market is μ.

Under the premise of quality uncertainty, the decision basis for deciding whether to buy or not should be expected utility:

$$E(U_B) = c + tE(q)n = c + t\mu r$$

Here $E(q)$ reflects the expected quality level of Internet products, which is actually its average quality, that is, $\mu = E(q)$.

We substitute the budget constraint into the expected utility function as follows:

$$E(U_B) = Y_B + (t\mu - p)r$$

If you want to improve the utility of the buyer when purchasing the product, that is, $r = 1$, you should:

$$t\mu - p > 0, \text{ that is, } t\mu > p \text{ or } \mu > p/t \tag{3.3}$$

In fact, (3.3) shows us the decision boundary of the demand side.

3.2.2.3 The Possible Equilibrium Results Between the Supply and Demand Sides

Like Akerlof's [1] model, we base its supply–demand function on the relationship between average quality and price. According to Wilson [18, 19] model, the relationship between product price and average quality should be:

$$\mu = E(p|mq < p)$$

$$= \int_{q^0}^{p/m} qf(q)dq / S(p)$$

$$= \int_{q^0}^{p/m} qf(q)dq \bigg/ \int_{q^0}^{p/m} f(q)dq\left(q^0 < p < q^1\right) \tag{3.4}$$

Since it satisfies the conditions of (3.1) at the same time (3.4) actually shows the average quality level of the products that have reached the transaction, and more importantly, it shows the decision boundary of the supplier. By combining (3.4) with (3.3), we can analyze the transaction equilibrium condition between supply and demand sides, that is, Walrasian Equilibrium region.

In order to illustrate the problem, we give a certain probability distribution to the product quality. Assuming that q obeys a uniform distribution, its density function should be $f(q) = 1/(q^1 - q^0)$. Now, we discuss market equilibrium and price change in two cases according to the size of m:

[Case 1] $m = 1$, so (3.4) becomes:

$$\mu = \int_{q^0}^{p} \frac{q}{q^1 - q^0} dq \bigg/ \int_{q^0}^{p} \frac{q}{q^1 - q^0} dq = \frac{p + q^0}{2} \tag{3.5}$$

Then, the possible equilibrium results between supply and demand sides are shown in Fig. 3.1.

In Fig. 3.1, formula (3.4) expresses ray $S(q^0 > 0)$ and ray $S(q^0 = 0)$, which are two supply curves with different starting points of mass distribution, and reflect the decision-making willingness and basis of the supplier. Equation (3.3) expressed in Fig. 3.1 is the lower right of ray $D(t \geq 1)$, which is the decision boundary of the demander. As described above, in order to ensure that the transaction can be carried

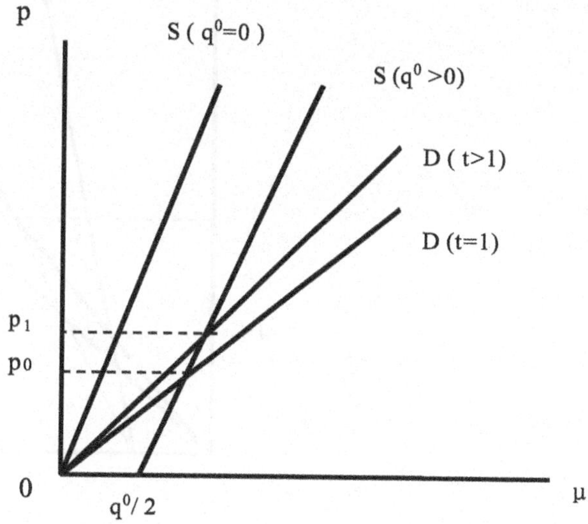

Fig. 3.1 The possible equilibrium results between supply and demand sides ($m = 1$)

out smoothly, it is necessary to have $t \geq 1$, so the ray $D\,(t = 1)$ is the lowest boundary of all ray clusters $D(t \geq 1)$ expressing requirements. Obviously, the intersection of supply region and demand region is Walras equilibrium region. This intersection is the intersection of the lower right region of curve D and ray S.

If the lowest mass of the Internet product is zero ($q^0 = 0$), the intersection of the corresponding lower right region of $S(q^0 = 0)$ and $D(t \geq 1)$, that is, the only possible equilibrium, is the origin (0, 0), which has no practical significance and can be ignored.

Now let's look at the case where the lowest mass is non-zero (that is, $q^0 > 0$). From Fig. 3.1, we can see that if the consumer makes up for his lack of quality judgment by reducing his preference for the quality of Internet products due to the virtuality of the Internet (t value will approach 1 more), it is reflected in the figure that the boundary forming equilibrium will narrow and the reflected equilibrium price will drop (from p^1 to p^0 in the figure). This shows that due to the virtuality of the Internet, the Internet market is easy to form a low-price equilibrium.

[Case 2] If $m \neq 1$, then (3.4) becomes:

$$\mu = \int_{q^0}^{p/m} \frac{q}{q^1 - q^0} dq \Big/ \int_{q^0}^{p/m} \frac{1}{q^1 - q^0} dq = \frac{1}{2}\left(\frac{p}{m} + q^0\right) \tag{3.6}$$

Assuming that the seller's preference for product quality is $m \neq 1$, then when it is combined with Eq. (3.3), the possible equilibrium range between supply and demand sides is shown in Fig. 3.2.

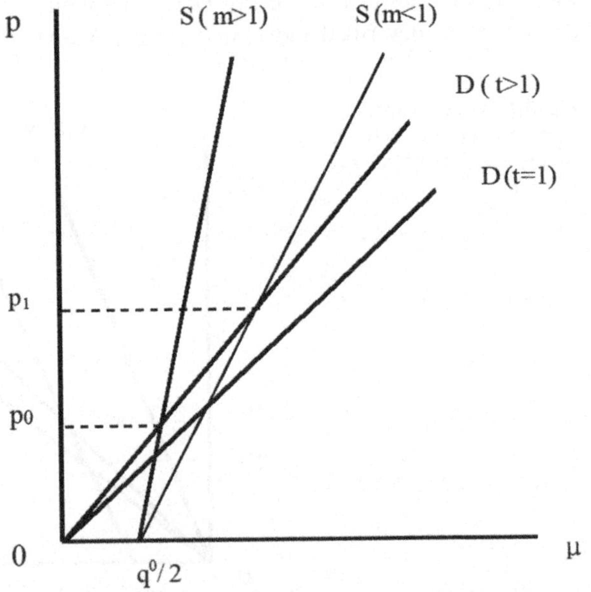

Fig. 3.2 The possible equilibrium results between supply and demand sides ($m \neq 1$)

From Fig. 3.2, we can see that with the increase of m, that is, when the potential Internet vendor's preference for product quality utility increases, the intersection of the supply area, that is, ray *S*, and the demand area, that is, the lower right of ray *D*, will shrink, which also means that the Walras equilibrium area is shrinking and the reflected equilibrium price will decrease (from p^1 to p^0 in the figure).

3.2.3 Basic Conclusions

From the above analysis, we can draw the following conclusions:

[Conclusion 1] The difference of preferences between buyers and sellers on product quality will lead to the narrowing of Walras equilibrium area and the decline of Walras equilibrium price. That is to say, in the Internet market, the difference of product quality preference between buyers and sellers will form a low-price equilibrium. The intuitive explanation of this phenomenon is that under the condition of Internet virtuality, consumers should not only try to understand the quality distribution of products, but also understand the sales motivation of sellers. Because of the virtual nature of the Internet, it will cause consumers' information disadvantage. Therefore, the 'lemon' problem reflected in the Internet market is more serious than the traditional market to some extent, or in other words, the 'lemon sensitivity' of Internet consumers is stronger.

[Conclusion 2] Because the market may approach the equilibrium of low price, the optimal solution of Multiple-Walrasian Equilibrium or Multiple-Pareto Criterion demonstrated by Wilson [18, 19] and Rose [14] will behave as multiple equilibrium of low price. Therefore, the strength of quality signal reflected by Internet product price is lower than that in traditional market. It can be inferred that we need to use more methods besides price to solve the 'lemon' problem in the Internet market, such as intermediary, signal and reputation.

[Conclusion 3] If a market is balanced at a low-price level, it may mean the decline of welfare level in market transactions and the failure of spontaneous coordination in the market. Therefore, compared with the physical market, the Internet market calls for the emergence of market coordinators. This coordinator may be a non-economic means such as quality intermediary or system as a third party.

[Conclusion 4] The quality distribution of Internet products will have an impact on the equilibrium results. At the extreme, if the minimum quality of a Internet product is assumed to be zero, the whole transaction may completely collapse. Only when the quality of the worst product is greater than zero can market equilibrium have practical significance. This also shows that if there are many inferior products in the Internet market, the possibility of market disintegration will be greater. Therefore, compared with the physical market, it is more important and necessary to standardize the e-commerce market.

[Conclusion 5] In essence, the root cause of the 'lemon' problem in the Internet market lies in the differences in consumption preferences and strategic behaviors between consumers and Internet enterprises. Although the Internet-based market provides a way to reduce transaction costs, it does not change the information asymmetry in market transactions. This is the premise for us to observe and use the Internet market.

3.2.4 *The Verification of the Basic Model*

Verification (I): American Coinage Internet Auction Market—Performance of Internet 'Gresham's law'

Huston and Spence's [10] survey of the US coinage Internet auction market provides a validation of our theoretical model. Huston and Spence pointed out that the reason why the coinage Internet auction market was chosen to verify the 'Internet lemon' problem is that it has a large transaction volume, on the other hand, it has multiple quality level distributions, and it is possible to rely on information to reduce uncertainty for easy observation.[5]

3.2.4.1 Mass Measurement

Assume that q_m is the highest quality that buyers can get. q_m is measured in US dollars, and market value is the logical standard of quality. There are two ways to measure q_m:

1. If the MARKET has the quality claimed by the seller, MARKET is a retail price.
2. Grade G of coinage. Coin collectors and dealers will grade coins to reflect their quality. These quality grades range from Poor-1 (so badly damaged that they can hardly be identified and measured) to MS-70—a 'mint-state' coin—'a coin that has not been in circulation at all', and mint-state produces coins with grades ranging from 60 to 70. In order to fully express the level of quality, Coin Universe Price Guide designed nine binary variables (equal to 0 or 1): if the coin is 'specially colored', GEF = 1, otherwise it is 0; GAU = 1 if the coin is 'probably not circulated', otherwise it is 0; if the coin is not in circulation, the mass of MS60, G60 = 1, otherwise it is 0; if the coin is not in circulation, the mass of MS62, G62 = 1, otherwise it is 0; if the coin is not in circulation, the mass of MS63, G63 = 1, otherwise it is 0; if the coin is not in circulation, the mass of MS64, G64 = 1, otherwise it is 0; if the coin is not in circulation, the mass of MS65, G65 = 1, otherwise it is 0; if the coin is not in circulation, the mass of MS66, G66 = 1, otherwise it is 0; if the coin is not in circulation, the mass of MS67, G67 = 1, otherwise it is 0.

---

[5] The main data of this verification comes from eBay website. The figures include an eBay auction of 225 Morgan models (stand-alone avatars) in US dollars, which took place in mid-May 2000. Such coins are chosen because their properties can be better described with relatively small errors.

3.2.4.2 Buyer's Information Variables

The set of information variables available to the buyer is: if the coinage is approved by the major coinage rating service,[6] CERT = 1; OTHER = 1 if coinage is rated by less well-known rating services; if a PICTURE contains a description of the item, PICTURE = 1.

3.2.4.3 EBay's Evaluation of the Transaction Results

eBay evaluates a seller based on the number of transactions he trades and the percentage of buyers who rate him positively. Then, the company gives the sellers stars of various colors based on their evaluation. If a seller is rated below 10, there is no star, 10–99 has a yellow star, and 100–499 has an emerald star. SELL = 0 if the seller is in the lowest range (no stars); SELL = 1 if the seller is in the next highest range; SELL = 2, if the seller is in the scope of the above catalog.

3.2.4.4 Results

The results of the regression analysis show the determinants of the likelihood of an item being sold and are listed in Table 3.1. The independent variable is SOLD, which is equal to 1 if it is a SOLD item; otherwise, it is equal to 0.

Dependency SOLD = 1, if coins are SOLD; otherwise 0.

$$SOLD = \beta_1 + \beta_2 MARKET + \beta_3 CERT + \beta_4 OTHER + \beta_5 PIC + \beta_6 SELL + \beta_7 GEF + \beta_8 GAU + \beta_9 G60 + \beta_{10} G62 + \beta_{11} G63 + \beta_{12} G64 + \beta_{13} G65 + \beta_{14} G65 + \varepsilon$$

In the above regression analysis, the coefficient of MARKET is negative, and the significance level is 5%, which indicates that high-quality goods are less likely to be sold. The coefficient of 'probably not flowing through' GAU level is negative, and its significance implies that this level is less likely to be sold than the lower VF level. The coefficient of the 'mint-state' level is negative, and as its level increases, the coefficient becomes larger and more significant. The G66 coefficient is not significant because there is a relatively large standard error resulting from a small number of coins of this grade. Three of the four information variables have a statistical significance of 10% or higher. Only PICTURE cannot explain any variables in sales.

The results show that high-quality coins are less easy to sell than low-quality coins. This is actually the Internet 'lemon' at work, and it is the performance of

[6] Because of the difficulty in determining the seigniorage, some companies began to provide rating services. In order to get a certain fee, the companies will have a team of professional raters, who set the level of coinage. Coins and labels indicating their grades are sealed in a plastic plate to ensure that the coins are kept in a certain state. Third-party rating agencies will provide buyers with more valuable information.

Table 3.1 Results of regression analysis of factors influencing sales

Variable name	Estimated parameter	Asymptotic value of T-ratio
MARKET	−0.002	−2.085**
CERT	0.492	2.014**
OTHER	−0.775	−0.746*
PIC	−0.199	−0.819
SELL	−0.317	−3.495***
GEF	0.005	0.010
GAU	−1.306	−3.282***
G60	−0.372	−0.828
G62	−0.425	−0.801
G63	−0.771	−1.828*
G64	−0.982	−2.387**
G65	−1.130	−2.451**
G66	−6.084	−0.0391
Constant	1.923	4.210***

Note * = Significance level is 10%; ** = Significance level is 5%; *** = Significance level is 1%); $N = 225$ observed values; likelihood ratio test = 53.7780; determination coefficient $R^2 = 0.2126$

the Internet trade 'Gresham Theorem' in the market. Because buyers suspect that sellers can provide goods of lower quality than they claim. The results also suggest that certification of important coinage grading services can improve the likelihood of sales by improving the information capabilities of potential buyers. Coins that have been identified are more likely to be sold. Not only does an unknown certification company have a lower value to the buyer, but it actually reduces the likelihood of a sale. The SELL (Seller's Experience) coefficient is negative, indicating that experienced sellers do not necessarily SELL more coins, because new buyers may be alert to experienced sellers.

In addition, Huston and Spence's survey also found that the price paid by buyers on the Internet is 78% of the wholesale price. This means that if coins are not sold directly to buyers but auctioned by dealers on the Internet, the marginal revenue of prices will drop significantly. For uncertified coins, which are most affected by the lemon problem, their average price is below 24.8% of the wholesale price. For certified coinage, consumers trust it very much, and its price is 20.0% lower than the retail price. (Certified mints with pictures are still below 19.2% of the retail price.) This result shows that information asymmetry, which discourages consumers, is an important reason for the low price of the Internet compared with the wholesale price.

Huston and Spence also found through calculations that although the price of coins sold increased with the increase in quality, the seller's claim to increase the quality by one dollar only increased the price by 87 cents. This fact shows that consumers will discount the quality improvement claimed by sellers. Compared with their market value, high-quality coins are often traded at a low price.

Verification (II): Internet books, CDs and other markets.

In terms of prices in the Internet market, the most thoroughly researched Internet products are books and CDs, because they are some of the first products to be marketed. The research work of Brynjolfsson and Smith [5] also validates the results of our previous model analysis to some extent. This result shows that compared with the traditional market, the price of Internet products is lower.

They chose books and CDs as their research objects. Brynjolfsson and Smith [5] point out that the focus on similar products is due to the high likelihood that they will be highly competitive in a given Internet distribution channel [3]. In this way, the impact of unobserved heterogeneity can be greatly reduced, and the differences between these two channels can be clearly measured. For each product, Brynjolfsson and Smith chose eight Internet retailers and eight traditional retailers, of which half were 'hybrid': they could choose between the Internet market and the traditional market. In the selection of Internet retailers, Brynjolfsson and Smith selected the four largest Internet retailers and the four largest hybrid retailers by using the statistics of website click-through rate of Web21. The four largest Internet retailers account for 99.8% of the Internet book market and 96.5% of the Internet CD retail market respectively.

Brynjolfsson and Smith [5] studied the performance of the book and CD market in terms of market efficiency indicators from 1998 to 1999, and found that the price in the Internet market is 9–16% lower than that in the traditional market, and even after considering transportation and handling, distribution and local taxes, it is still lower than that in the traditional market.

They analyzed the main features of an Internet marketplace that uses the Internet as a distribution channel (which mainly sells two similar but different products—books and CDs). They collected more than 8500 price observations over a 15-month period and compared the price behavior of 41 Internet and traditional retailers (see Table 3.2).

Through their T-tests on the hypothesis that the Internet average price (and average complete price) is lower than the offline average price (and average complete price) in two markets, the results fully verify their hypotheses (as shown in Tables 3.3 and 3.4).

In addition, Clay et al. [6]'s empirical research on the book market also came to the same conclusion—the online book price is lower or the same as the offline book price.

Table 3.2 Data collected by Brynjolfsson and Smith 1998.2–1999.3

Products	Number of retailers	Species	Observation value	Data source
Books	4(Internet)	20	1144	Internet
	4(Internet-Mixed)	20	1124	Internet
	4(Traditional-Mixed)	20	1111	Traditional market
	4(Traditional)	20	1037	Traditional market
CD	4(Internet)	20	1115	Internet
	4(Internet-Mixed)	20	1102	Internet
	4(Internet-Mixed)	20	1109	Traditional market
	4(Traditional)	20	978	

Table 3.3 *t*-test of average price

Product market	Traditional market Average price	Internet market average price	Hypothesis	*t* test for significance
Books	13.90	11.74	$P_{\text{INET}} < P_{\text{PHYS}}$	0.001
CD	16.07	13.49	$P_{\text{INET}} < P_{\text{PHYS}}$	0.001

Table 3.4 *t*-test for average complete price

Product market	Traditional market Average price	Internet market average price	Hypothesis	t test for significance
Books	15.04	13.69	$P_{\text{INET}} < P_{\text{PHYS}}$	0.001
CD	17.41	15.15	$P_{\text{INET}} < P_{\text{PHYS}}$	0.001

3.3 Extension of Theoretical Model: Adverse Selection and Market Segmentation

Through the previous basic theoretical model, we analyze the influence of the Internet 'lemon' problem on the Internet market equilibrium. We may have such a question: Since the Internet market is prone to low-price equilibrium, what impact will this equilibrium have on the traditional market? Now, we use the theoretical analysis model of Internet adverse selection to analyze the market segmentation and equilibrium between traditional market (physical market) and Internet market.

We represent the type of market with *i*, which is a discrete binary variable $i = \{N, M\}$, *N* represents the Internet market and *M* represents the traditional market. The quality of Internet products is represented by $q_i \in [q_i^0, q_i^1]$, and its quality distribution function is $f(q_i)$. We first establish the demand function and supply function of two markets:

3.3.1 The Seller

For the seller, his utility function is:

$$U_s^i = Y_s^i + (m^i - p)n \tag{3.7}$$

Here, $n = \{0, 1\}$ is also a discrete binary variable, which indicates whether the seller sells the product, $n = 1$ means not selling the product, and $n = 0$ means selling the product. It is a utility index, which reflects the seller's evaluation of the quality of Internet products. Because it is the absolute price, not the relative price, that affects the decision, we define the price of the product as *p* and the price of other goods as 1. Y_s^i is the vendor's budget constraint.

If you want to improve the utility of the seller when selling the product, that is, $n = 0$, you should:

$$m^i q_i - p < 0, \text{ that is } m^i q_i < p \text{ or } q_i < \frac{p}{m^i} \tag{3.8}$$

Then, at any price, meet the condition $q_i < \frac{p}{m^i}$ the proportion of products:

$$S(p) = prob\left(q_i < \frac{p}{m^i}\right) = \int_{q_0}^{p/m^i} f(q_i)dq_i (m^i q_i^0 < p) \tag{3.9}$$

3.3.2 *The Buyer*

For the buyer, under the premise of quality uncertainty, the decision-making basis of whether he buys or not should be expected utility. Assume that his expected utility for products purchased in two markets is:

$$E(U_B^i) = Y_B + (t^i \mu^i - p)r \tag{3.10}$$

Again, here $r = \{0, 1\}$ is a discrete binary variable, $r = 1$ for buying, and $r = 0$ for not buying; t^i represents the relative evaluation parameter of the quality of Internet products compared with the consumption of other goods, like the original basic assumption. To ensure that the transaction can be carried out, it should be $t^i \geq m^i$. We also use p to represent the quality of products, while the price of other goods is defined as 1. $E(q)$ reflects the expected quality level of Internet products, which is actually its average quality, that is, $\mu^i = E(q)$. Y_B is the budget revenue for the buyer.

If you want to improve the utility of the buyer when purchasing the product, that is, $r = 1$, you should:

$$t^i \mu^i - p > 0, \text{ that is } t^i \mu^i > p, \text{ or } \mu^i > \frac{p}{t^j} \tag{3.11}$$

Equation (3.11) actually shows us the decision boundary of the demand side.

3.3.3 The Equilibrium Conditions of the Two Markets

Whether consumers buy products in the traditional market or the Internet market depends on the size of $E(U_B^i)$. We can discuss it in three situations:

1. In order to make consumers willing to buy products in the physical market, they should:

$$E(U_B^M) > E(U_B^N) \tag{3.12}$$

2. To make consumers willing to buy products in the Internet market, they should:

$$E(U_B^M) < E(U_B^N) \tag{3.13}$$

3. In order for consumers to be willing to buy products in both markets, they should:

$$E(U_B^M) = E(U_B^N) \tag{3.14}$$

According to Wilson's basic model [19], the relationship between product price and average quality in two markets should be:

$$\begin{aligned}\mu^i &= E\left(p \middle| m^i q_i < p\right)\\ &= \int_{q^0}^{p/m^i} q_i f(q_i) dq_i / S(p)\\ &= \int_{q^0}^{p/m^i} q_i f(q_i) dq \bigg/ \int_{q^0}^{p/m^i} (q_i) dq_i \left(q_1^0 < p < q_i^1\right)\end{aligned} \tag{3.15}$$

Equation (3.15) actually shows the average quality level of the products that are concluded, and it shows us the decision boundary of the supplier side.

Now, we assume that the quality of products obeys an even distribution in the two markets, then

$$\mu^i = \int_{q^0}^{p/m^2} \frac{q_i}{q_i^1 - q_i^0} dq_i / \int_{q^0}^{p/m^i} \frac{1}{q_i^1 - q_i^0} dq = \frac{1}{2}\left(p\frac{p}{m^i} + q_i^0\right) \tag{3.16}$$

Combining these conditions, we can get three market 'separation equilibrium' conditions:

4. Market equilibrium conditions for the completion of transactions in the physical market:

$$t^M \mu^M > t^N \mu^N \tag{3.17}$$

$$\mu^M = \frac{1}{2}\left(\frac{p}{m^M} + q^0\right) \tag{3.18}$$

$$\mu^M > \frac{p}{t^M} \tag{3.19}$$

5. Market equilibrium conditions for transactions to be completed in the Internet market:

$$t^M \mu^M < t^N \mu^N \tag{3.20}$$

$$\mu^N = \frac{1}{2}\left(\frac{p}{m^N} + q^0\right) \tag{3.21}$$

$$\mu^N > \frac{p}{t^N} \tag{3.22}$$

6. Market equilibrium conditions under which transactions can be completed in any market:

$$t^M \mu^M = t^N \mu^N \tag{3.23}$$

$$\mu^i = \frac{1}{2}\left(\frac{p}{m^i} + q^0\right) \tag{3.24}$$

$$\mu^i > \frac{p}{t^i} \tag{3.25}$$

By comparing (IV) and (V), we can find that the market in which the transaction takes place ultimately depends on the relationship $t^M \mu^M$ with $t^N \mu^N$ and the decision boundary of the demand side.

3.3.4 Conclusion

The physical market and the e-commerce market are divided according to the average quality and the quality preference of market participants, and the interaction between them. With the quality uncertainty, the persistent adverse selection problem is induced, and a 'separated' equilibrium may appear between the e-commerce market and the traditional market. However, with the decrease of Internet 'lemon', the substitution of e-commerce market for traditional market will be enhanced.

3.3.5 Verification: German Automobile Market

Fabel and Lehmann [13] once analyzed the sales situation of German cars in two markets.

They chose two types of cars sold in the German automobile market: Volkswagen Rabbits III series and BMW 3 series. BMW series is more favored by people who love automobile sports, and the price is higher; the VW Rabbit is a typical economical car with a lower price. These two models are very popular in Germany and are sold through traditional market and Internet market. All the data they collected spanned from June 1999 to January 2000. Of the 981 sample points for the two brands, 393 were taken from traditional markets (see Table 3.5 for statistical results).

Fabel and Lehmann's statistical analysis shows that the lower average electronic price has a higher trading tendency in the low-quality market, that is to say, the Internet trading occurs more in the low-quality cars. We can see from the table that there is a big difference in automobile engines between the two markets. Therefore, despite the advantages of Internet search methods, these two markets will coexist. The difference lies not in the car brand, but in the quality gap of each brand car and the gap between buyers and sellers' understanding of it.

3.4 The Theoretical Explanation: Internet Adverse Selection and Solutions

In the previous section, we constructed the basic theoretical model of the Internet 'lemon market'. From the conclusion of the model, we can see that the Internet market is easy to achieve equilibrium at the low-price level, which means the decline of welfare level in market transactions and the failure of spontaneous coordination

Table 3.5 Statistical results of quality samples in two markets

Variable	Traditional market		Internet market	
	Average (Median)	Maximum value (Minimum)	Average (Median)	Maximum value (Minimum)
Car ceiling	0. 37 (n.a.)	1(0)	0. 55 (n.a.)	1(0)
Safety bag	0. 38 (n.a.)	1(0)	0. 49 (n.a.)	1(0)
Air conditioner	0. 40 (n.a.)	1(0)	0. 20 (n.a.)	1(0)
Engine size	1.7(1.6)	2.8(1.4)	1.8(1.3)	3.5(1.4)
Horsepower	99(101)	192(60)	109(102)	217(60)
Usage time (months)	44.6(40.0)	180.0(1.0)	77.2(73)	228.0(4.0)
Total mileage (km)	57,813(56,000)	165,000 (100)	96,962 (95,000)	266,000 (200)
Monthly mileage (km)	1333 (1225)	8929 (100)	1393 (1229)	8928 (25)
Price	23,745 (22,800)	51,500 (1500)	16,599 (16,000)	59,500 (700)

in the market. Although the emergence and rapid development of e-commerce is considered to reflect the advantages of information environment and imply the substitution of traditional market, due to the serious adverse selection problem existing in the Internet market, it will have an adverse impact on the efficiency of transactions. Therefore, trying to reduce the 'lemon' problem in the Internet market is an inevitable requirement for us to give full play to the efficiency of the e-commerce market. More importantly, because the strength of quality signal reflected by Internet product price is lower than that of traditional market, we should pay special attention to the role of reputation means, intermediary means and non-economic means in solving Internet adverse selection.

Now, based on the conclusion of the basic theoretical model, we put forward a relatively complete idea to solve the adverse selection problem in the Internet market.

Let's start with the methods and ways to solve the 'lemon' problem in the traditional market.

3.4.1 The Traditional Market Solves the Problem of Adverse Selection

As far as traditional market is concerned, adverse selection leads to market failure or inefficiency of market operation, which makes market participants have to use various possible methods or solutions to improve market efficiency, thus making the market paralyzed by asymmetric information run again. There are roughly the following ways to solve the 'lemon' problem in the traditional market:

3.4.1.1 According to the Price of Goods to Guess the Quality of Goods

Because the 'lemon' principle tells us that in an asymmetric information environment, commodity quality depends on price, that is to say, high price means high quality. Therefore, to some extent, we can use the price as a signal to transmit and judge the quality.[7] However, whether price can be used as a quality signal seems to depend on other available information. For example, Szybillo and Jacoby [17] pointed out that the difference of actual product quality and the image of stores will make price not an important product quality indicator. This leads to the emergence of other ways and means.

---

[7] In fact, some scholars have given other explanations about this point. For example, Scitovszky [15] thinks that consumers can use price as a sign of product quality, because higher price means that the input production factors are more expensive and the cost is higher, so the product quality is better. Frank [7] believes that when the cost of information collection is high and the cognitive processing ability is limited, consumers can only rely on price to judge the quality.

3.4.1.2 Manufacturing and Disseminating Market Signals

In the traditional market, the method of manufacturing and disseminating market signaling is the most important and commonly used means, which mainly makes consumers distinguish their products from 'lemon' by means of brand, advertisement or providing quality guarantee, warranty and return to customers, so as to believe that their products are of high quality.

Brand is a name, term, mark, symbol, pattern, or a combination of these factors, which is used to identify the manufacturer and seller of products. Akerlof [1] once pointed out in his classic paper that 'brand can not only show the quality of products, but also provide consumers with a series of retaliatory measures when the quality of products fails to meet the expected requirements, because consumers can reduce the amount of purchases in the future. Moreover, new products are often associated with old brands, which can guarantee the quality of products to its future consumers'. Therefore, a brand should be a promise made by the seller to continuously provide a series of product features, benefits and services to the buyer. For example, Chrysler Motor Company of the United States promised to provide a five-year and 50,000-mile warranty for its cars, which shows that the company has confidence in its products. Consumers can speculate that if the manufacturer is willing to provide such warranty, the cars it sells must be of high quality. For another example, a manufacturer can be willing to buy its products by establishing stores and warranty shops with high scale and grade, so that consumers can judge the quality of goods from the elegant appearance of the store environment or the seller's logo.

The research on how economic actors compensate for adverse selection has taken up a large part of the incomplete market research literature. One of the most important points in this research was put forward by Spence [16], who pointed out that sellers of high-quality products try to show themselves by undertaking certain activities that are cheaper for them than sellers of low-quality products. In his example, more production workers use their educational background to show their productivity. In the product market, enterprises use guarantee to show the reliability of their product quality. In the credit market, lenders use collateral to show their credibility [4].

3.4.1.3 Intermediary

Intermediary uses its professional knowledge to provide information for buyers, and through it, it can 'match' buyers and sellers, such as brokers and brokers. Of course, the income of an intermediary depends on the quality of information it provides.

3.4.1.4 Means in a Non-strict Economic Sense

This means mainly refers to the government, consumer associations, etc. through this standard to ensure the quality of products. Strictly speaking, this method should be a non-economic solution.

3.4.1.5 Search

The method of searching is that consumers change their adverse selection status through their own information search, such as visiting, investigating, searching letters and so on.

3.4.1.6 Providing Incomplete Contracts

The so-called incomplete contract means that the buyer and the seller only make rough or ambiguous provisions on some clauses or responsibilities signed, and once the product quality problems occur, the contract will be terminated forever. Incomplete contracts here provide a penalty and incentive mechanism, which urges suppliers to provide high-quality products. In other words, the reward for high-quality products is the continuation of the contract. Once the existence of low-quality products is discovered, the contract will be terminated. Although this method first appeared in traditional transactions, it is also used as a method to reduce adverse selection in Internet trade.

3.4.1.7 The Establishment of Quality Standards

In the traditional market, the government, consumer associations and so on often establish the qualified standard of product quality, and ensure the quality of products through this standard. However, in fact, the quality qualification standard only puts forward the minimum requirements for the product and indicates whether the product can be used, rather than a quality standard. Therefore, it can not guarantee the quality of the product, but it can also be regarded as a method to reduce adverse selection.

3.4.2 The Possible Methods to Solve the Internet Adverse Selection

As mentioned in the previous section, because the 'lemon' problem in the Internet market and the 'lemon' problem in the traditional market have different characteristics and performances, it also determines that the means or ways to solve the 'lemon' in the Internet will be different.

Based on the conclusion of the basic theoretical model, we will summarize the ways to solve the 'lemon' problem in the Internet market according to the comparison with the traditional market.

3.4.2.1 According to the Price of Goods to Guess the Quality of Goods

Although in the traditional market, we use the price as a signal to pass and judge the quality to some extent. However, in the Internet market, this method is difficult to apply. Because the theoretical model has told us that the signaling quality through prices will be weak in the Internet market. Therefore, in the Internet market, we need to use other methods to solve the 'lemon' problem, such as intermediary, signal and reputation.

3.4.2.2 Manufacturing and Disseminating Market Signals

In the traditional market, manufacturing and disseminating market signals is the most important and commonly used means in the traditional market. Consumers can distinguish their products from 'lemon' by means of brand, advertisement or providing quality guarantee, warranty and return to customers, so as to believe that their products are of high quality. However, in the e-commerce market, there will be new difficulties in manufacturing and disseminating market signals: (1) If the Internet market sells digital products, it is difficult to disclose the quality of information products but not their true contents when manufacturing and disseminating market signals. (2) The measures taken in the traditional market to guarantee the quality of products, such as unconditional return policy, are difficult to realize in the Internet market. This is because if the Internet market sells digital products, it is easy to copy. In fact, the 'returned' products are meaningless; second, a refund is also not feasible, because in the case of buying low-value items, the disposal cost is much higher than the value of the items. (3) As an indirect information, signals are transmitted to consumers through identification and reputation. However, this approach builds on what consumers do when they repeat their purchases, and reputable companies have little advantage when consumers do not repeat their purchases. (4) In the traditional market, manufacturers may set up shops and warranty shops with high scale and grade, so that consumers can judge the quality of goods from the elegant appearance of the shop environment or the seller's logo, so that they are willing to buy the products of the manufacturer. However, in the Internet market of e-commerce, these indirect signals can not be provided or change frequently. Therefore, the indirect signals available in the traditional market may not be effective in the Internet market. In fact, according to the latest statistics of T*he 12th Statistical Report on Internet Development in China* issued by China Internet Information Center (CNNIC), the main way for consumers to know new websites is search engine (accounting for about 46%), and only a small part is known through Internet advertisements of enterprises.

However, it should be emphasized that the role of price display quality will be weak in the Internet market. Therefore, the method of manufacturing and spreading market signals, such as reputation method, as the main way to solve the adverse selection of the market, is still a very important method in the Internet market, but its expression and utilization will be different. For example, the Internet market can use the traditional reputation to spread and extend, and the technical conditions of the

Internet can endow the Internet market with some new methods, so that we can use the Internet reputation to establish Internet trust. We will discuss the specific content in the fourth chapter.

3.4.2.3 Intermediary

The Internet 'lemon market' model tells us that the Internet market may need market coordinators more. As a market coordinator, intermediary can play a relatively large role in solving adverse selection in the Internet market. The application and operation mechanism of quality in solving Internet adverse selection will be discussed in detail in the fifth chapter of this paper.

3.4.2.4 Means in a Non-strict Economic Sense

Like the intermediary method, we know from the previous theoretical model that compared with the physical market, the e-commerce market calls for the emergence of market coordinator, and this coordinator may also be a non-economic means. In the Internet market, we should pay more attention to its effect. In the sixth chapter, we will expand this problem and discuss the role of non-economic means in solving the Internet 'lemon' problem.

3.4.2.5 Seeking

This method is an advantage given by the Internet to participants in the Internet market. Consumers can take advantage of the incomparably powerful transmission and search advantages on the Internet to change their information disadvantages, which is also an effective way to avoid the 'lemon' problem, such as using search engines (web), Usenet newsgroups and so on. Compared with the search methods in the traditional market, the search cost in the Internet market is much lower. But it must be pointed out that even so, the information obtained by consumers is still incomplete. For example, Gallaugher and Downing [8] studied several famous search engines and found that in December 1997, the coverage rate of search engines was only over 20%, while in February 1999, the coverage rate of no search engine exceeded 16%. Moreover, as the number of pages available on the World Wide Web increases dramatically, coverage will decline.[8]

[8] This data is quoted from: Jeikiy [11].

3.4.2.6 Providing Incomplete Contracts

Although this method appears in traditional transactions, it can also be used as a method to reduce adverse selection in Internet trade. Because their essence is the same: incomplete contract provides a mechanism combining punishment and incentive mechanism, which can urge suppliers to provide high-quality products to avoid the emergence of Internet 'lemon'.

3.4.2.7 The Establishment of Quality Standards

The role and effect of this method in the Internet market is no different from that in the traditional market. In fact, the quality qualification standard only puts forward the minimum requirements for the product, indicating whether the product can be used, rather than a quality standard, so it cannot guarantee the quality of the product. But it can still be used as a way to reduce the Internet 'lemon' problem.

In addition, there are some solutions to adverse selection in the Internet market, which are not available in the traditional market. For example, the method of bundling sales, the method of providing Internet free trial and attention sales, etc.

These methods will be analyzed according to the corresponding contents in the fourth chapter.

3.4.3 The Problems That Need to Be Explained

It should be pointed out that no matter in the traditional market or the Internet market, there are some methods to make the inefficient market due to adverse selection regain the market efficiency. However, all these methods are faced with the problem of failure. For example, when consumers only judge the quality according to the price of products, it may lead businesses to take advantage of the buyer's psychology and only raise the price without improving the quality unilaterally. In addition, when consumers search, they have to spend certain search costs (including technical costs and time costs, etc.), which they sometimes can't afford. Therefore, market participants and economists are constantly looking for or designing various methods to reduce the adverse effects of information asymmetry on themselves. However, the failure of the method may cause the market that regains efficiency to fall into a new round of efficiency cycle. When the problems caused by asymmetric information, such as adverse selection and moral hazard, generally exist in the economic system, it is difficult for people to believe that they can achieve pareto optimal efficiency, but only pareto suboptimal efficiency. Although it has lower entry barriers and higher information acquisition efficiency in the Internet market, it does not mean that the Internet market will be able to obtain higher market transaction efficiency.

Grossman and Stiglitz [9] put forward an important conclusion called 'Grossman-Stiglitz paradox' in their article 'On the impossibility of information efficient markets', which is composed of two proven contradictory propositions: ① If the price information in the market is fully transmitted, then the market equilibrium does not exist; ② if there is a price to pay for obtaining information, there will be no competitive equilibrium in the usual sense. The paradox of 'equilibrium' derived from the above two conclusions completely denies the premise that the information implied in traditional economics is fully transmitted. In fact, if market participants can obtain the required market information without paying the cost, then no one will search for and transmit information, but the market may make it difficult for market participants to have information differences because of the noise-free and efficient dissemination of information, and no one has the motivation to collect and disseminate information, thus making it difficult for the market to cultivate trading opportunities and reduce market efficiency. This paradox shows us from the opposite side that complete information cannot effectively improve market efficiency, on the contrary, it may hinder the exertion of market efficiency. Extremely high and extremely low information acquisition and transmission efficiency will hinder the improvement of market efficiency. Of course, information economics does not tell us to what extent the efficiency of information should be maintained, but we can be sure that the incompleteness or asymmetry of market information is not only a reality, but also a necessity—this is the premise for us to solve the problem of Internet adverse selection.

Therefore, it is impossible to hope to eliminate the asymmetry of quality information fundamentally, but strive to reduce or reduce the influence of information asymmetry on the transaction efficiency of Internet market—this should also be the most basic goal of our research on Internet adverse selection.

References

1. Akerlof GA (1970) The market for 'lemon': qualitative uncertainty and the market mechanism. Quart J Econ 84(3):488–500
2. Arrow KJ (1970) Essays in the theory of risk bearing. Markham, Chicago
3. Bakos JY (1997) Reducing buyer search costs: implications for electronic marketplaces. Manage Sci 43:1676–1692
4. Bester H (1984) Screening versus rationing in credit markets with imperfect information. University of Bonn Discussion Paper No. 136, May
5. Brynjolfsson E, Smith M (2000) Frictionless commerce? A comparison of internet and conventional retailers. Manage Sci 46:563–585
6. Clay K, Krishnan R, Wolff E, Fernandes D (2000) Retail strategies on the web: price and non-price competition in the online book industry. Carnegie Mellon University, Mimeo
7. Frank RH (1991) Microeconomics and behavior. McGraw-Hill Inc., New York
8. Gallaugher, Downing (1999) Market leadership and the web portal industry: an empirical investigation. Working Paper, Boston College
9. Grossman SJ, Stiglitz JE (1980) On the impossibility of informational efficient markets. Am Econ Rev 70(3):393–408
10. Huston JH, Spence RW (2002) Quality, uncertainty and the internet: the market for cyber lemons. Am Econ 46(1):50–60
11. Jeikiy (2002) Internet market efficiency paradox: a new explanatory framework. World Economy 2:12–20

12. Molho I (1997) The economics of information: lying and cheating in markets and organizations. Blackwell, Oxford
13. Fabel O, Lehmann EE (2002) Adverse selection and market substitution by electronic trade. Int J Econ Bus 9(2):175–193
14. Rose C (1993) Equilibrium and adverse selection. Rand J Econ 24:559–569
15. Scitovszky T (1945) Some consequences of the habit of judging quality by price. Rev Econ Stud 12(Winter):100–105
16. Spence M (1973) Job market signaling. Quart J Econ 87(3):355–374
17. Szybillo GJ, Jacoby J (1974) Intrinsic versus extrinsic cues as determinants of perceived product quality. J Appl Psychol 59(February):74–78
18. Wilson C (1979) Equilibrium and adverse selection. Am Econ Rev 69(2):313–317
19. Wilson C (1980) The nature of equilibrium in markets with adverse selection. Bell J Econ 11:108–130

Chapter 4
Adverse Selection and Price Behavior in Internet Market

Although we explain in Chapter 3 that the internal mechanism of Internet price reflecting quality is not as obvious as that of traditional market, price is the eternal theme of market. Whether it is traditional marketing or Internet marketing, price competition is always a weapon that enterprises must use. Therefore, when we study the problem of Internet adverse selection, we must pay special attention to the behavior of Internet price.

Then, how to treat the price behavior of the Internet market under adverse selection is the problem we want to discuss in this chapter.

4.1 Product Prices and Characteristics of Internet Market

Price, in a narrow sense, is the money charged for products or services, and in a broad sense, it refers to the total value that consumers use to exchange the benefits of owning or using products or services. The traditional pricing method of marketing is cost additive method, which is extremely difficult in the Internet market, because the cost characteristics of Internet products are high development cost and low replication cost; The period cost is very high and the product cost is very low; The fixed cost is very high and the variable cost is very low; The sunk cost is very high and the cash cost is very low. Therefore, more Internet products use differential pricing methods to price Internet products.

Pricing strategy is the most flexible and artistic strategy of Internet marketing, an important component of enterprise marketing mix strategy, and a very important competitive means of enterprises. All for-profit or non-profit organizations must price their products or services. The formation of Internet marketing price is extremely complex, which is influenced and restricted by many factors. Generally speaking, the factors that affect the Internet pricing of enterprise products include traditional marketing factors and the factors that affect the price of the Internet itself. Among

Y. Pan, *Trust Management in the Chinese E-Commerce Market*,
Advanced Studies in E-Commerce, https://doi.org/10.1007/978-981-97-1115-4_4

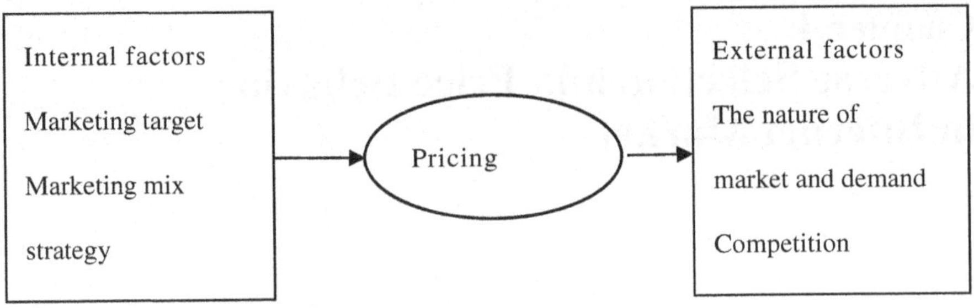

Fig. 4.1 Factors affecting the pricing of Internet products

them, traditional factors include internal (cost and profit, etc.) and external (consumer demand and market competition, etc.) (as shown in Fig. 4.1).

Judging from the current situation, the current pricing strategies in the Internet market mainly include:

1. Discrimination pricing strategy. This is the most commonly used method in Internet marketing at present. Discrimination pricing is to determine the price of digital products sold Internet according to the different degrees of satisfaction of consumers' needs. In addition to make it easier to personalize products, the Internet also makes it easier to personalize prices. In the traditional market, the mode of 'selling to everyone at one price' is generally adopted, but the technology adopted in Internet sales is 'peer-to-peer', and this strategy is 'one-to-one marketing'. We will make a special analysis on the influence of this strategy on adverse selection in the next section.
2. Penetration pricing strategy. To implement penetration pricing, it is necessary to adopt low price, zero price or negative price at the initial stage of entering the market, that is, to strike first, so as to strive for more installation foundation and reach the necessary critical value. Its purpose is to 'lock in' consumers, that is, to cultivate consumers' loyalty to products. Some digital products should adopt the strategy of selling at low price and zero price when entering the market. For example, Netscape Browser installed them on new machines at low price or even free gift when entering the market, thus obtaining a preconceived favorable position in the Internet browser market. Some digital products should adopt the strategy of negative price to compete for consumers. For example, some newly established websites often adopt the way of paying fees, linking their websites to well-known websites, so that users can browse their products through hyperlinks.
3. Market skimming pricing. This is a pricing strategy implemented at the mature stage of the market. After Internet products enter the mature stage of products, in order to effectively prevent competitors from entering, Internet enterprises can initially set high prices when new products appear. When the initial sales volume drops, or when competitors develop similar products, they must immediately reduce their prices in order to attract new customers who are sensitive to the price. In this way, although some short-term interests will be sacrificed,

it can achieve the purpose of occupying the market for a long time. The market skimming pricing method is suitable for products with technical advantages and difficult to be imitated by competitors in the short term.

4. Price leading pricing method. A price leader is a product competitor who launches a certain product at the lowest price. In the offline world, Wolmat is a price leader and a leader in retail. In the Internet market, this is a valuable strategy, but the competition is fierce and the price leader is fleeting. For example, Buy.com is the price leader of many commodities in America.
5. Segmented pricing. Many Internet companies adjust prices based on customers, geographic location or products. Companies that sell Internet and in retail stores must decide whether Internet prices are above, below or equal to offline prices. Internet prices are often lower, which in turn leads to channel conflicts. For example, in the United States, Networksolution.com has adopted a segmented pricing strategy in terms of domain name charges.
6. Dynamic pricing. XML and other technologies make dynamic web pages possible. These technologies enable database information to be organized on web pages. This means that the price information can be updated immediately and continuously after the new product features are developed and when the price adjustment of these products is decided. This information can change according to time and user.
7. Psychological pricing. Although marketers tend to weaken consumers' sensitivity to price by various differences and avoid vicious price-cutting competition, price has always had an important impact on consumer psychology. Whether this price method can be realized is greatly influenced by psychological factors.
8. Reference price. Adding high-priced product items in the Internet marketing product line virtually improves the reference price of consumers and makes other products on the product line seem cheap. Positioning a compromise product will enable you to gain more buyers. For example, providing extra technical support as a 'golden version' method will have little cost to increase as long as not many people choose the golden version.
9. Track pricing. By using the technical conditions of the Internet, such as Customer Tracking, we often pay attention to the needs of customers, and always pay attention to the changes in the needs and psychological changes of potential customers, so as to determine the price.
10. Brand pricing or reputation pricing. As mentioned in the previous chapter, a brand is a name, term, mark, symbol, design or a combination of these factors used to identify the manufacturer and seller of a product. It should be a promise made by the seller to continuously provide the buyer with a series of product features, benefits and services. Because consumers regard brand as an important part of products, brand building can increase the value of products. As mentioned earlier, brand, as a strong market signal, can reduce the information disadvantages faced by consumers in the market and adverse selection, and at the same time, it can reduce the search cost of consumers, which can benefit

consumers. Therefore, in the Internet marketing, the brand and quality of products will also become the factors affecting the price, which can have a great impact on customers.

From the above kinds of product pricing in the Internet market, we can see that due to the advanced efficiency of communication and exchange in the electronic market, Internet technology has brought extravagant hopes for Internet enterprises to set prices, which are almost impossible to realize in the traditional market. However, from an economic point of view, the asymmetric information problem ('lemon problem') brought by the inconsistent pricing in the Internet market also brings difficulties to judge whether the whole market is reasonable or not. We can get some enlightenment from the following cases and find some problems.

Case: Inspiration and Problems of Priceline.com **Pricing Marketing Model**[1]

Priceline.com's unique marketing method is to allow consumers to quote Priceline.com a price they are willing to pay for a certain product or service through the Internet, and the company is responsible for finding suppliers willing to sell the product at the price set by consumers from its own database or supplier network.[2] As soon as this pricing model appeared, it was favored by leisure tourists and airlines. Passengers quote the ticket price they are willing to pay, agree to be flexible in choosing airlines, departure times, stopovers and transit flights, keep their quotations valid for a certain period as required by the company, and guarantee them by credit card. Once the company finds a service provider during this period, customers cannot withdraw their quotations. A round-trip air ticket from New York to Los Angeles can cost as little as $300 to $350. For airlines, instead of leaving seats idle at the last minute, it is better to sell at low prices to increase revenue. As a result, the company attracted 1 million customers to its website in the first week of its official Internet operation, successfully sold 10,000 air tickets in the first six weeks, and ranked among the top ten most popular commercial websites in the United States. Since then, its business scale has been expanding continuously. In July 1998, it began to sell cars in the same way. In the first few days of market trials in New York, the sales volume exceeded 2 million yuan (Fig. 4.2).

Priceline.com's consumer pricing model stands out in the highly competitive US market because it reflects consumer sovereignty to some extent and benefits suppliers as well. It fully illustrates that the emergence of Internet enables manufacturers to implement certain price discrimination strategies. This is undoubtedly a leap in marketing concept.

However, this consumer pricing model has some defects: In the process of determining commodity prices, manufacturers are still in a dominant position, and

[1] Part of this case comes from Zhang Bin [4].

[2] Priceline.com was founded by Jay Walker. At present, the products sold by the company using the consumer pricing model include three categories: First, tourism service products such as air tickets, hotel rooms and car rental; Second, personal financing services such as housing mortgage, refinancing and mortgage loans and car sales business currently carried out in 13 States; Third, long-distance telephone service.

Fig. 4.2 Priceline.com web page

consumers are still at a disadvantage of information. Because in Priceline.com's consumer pricing system, there is a lower limit of the supply price of potential suppliers, and only the price quoted by consumers is above its lower limit can a transaction be made. Consumers have only a certain say in price, and the decision-making power is still in the hands of manufacturers. Therefore, although the Internet market has the advantage of marketing, it does not mean that consumers can obtain complete consumer surplus. One of the important reasons is that the information asymmetry between buyers and sellers has not been fundamentally changed in the Internet market, and consumers are still in the position of adverse selection.

4.2 Adverse Selection and Price Discrimination in Internet Market

4.2.1 *Introduction: The concept expression and basic conditions of price discrimination*

As for price discrimination, we often see it in real life. For example, when you call, the price varies greatly at different times. There are zero tickets and monthly tickets for rides, and tickets for tourist attractions are divided into off-season fares and peak season fares. At present, with the rapid development of Internet economy, price discrimination is used by Internet manufacturers as a modern marketing means. For example, 'one-to-one marketing', that is, selling to each user at different prices, is considered as a diversified and personalized modern marketing mode to meet consumers' needs.

So, what is price discrimination? There are many expressions about its concept. In *New Palgrey Economics Classic*,[3] price discrimination is defined as: 'Any time, two units of a commodity (by the same seller) are sold to two buyers at different competitive prices, there is price discrimination'. This definition is broad and can be understood as price discrimination in a broad sense. In *Microeconomics*, price discrimination is defined as: 'Price discrimination is to set different prices for different customers, sometimes for identical products, sometimes for products with slight differences'. This concept emphasizes that charging different prices for different customers for the same product is price discrimination. Mankiw gave a representative definition of price discrimination in a more concise way. He thought that price discrimination was the business practice of operators 'selling the same goods to different customers at different prices'. Mankiw believes that pure price discrimination can maximize the realization of producer surplus and help to improve social welfare.[4] In his book, *Theory of Industrial Organization*, Taylor expressed price discrimination as: 'When the price of the same commodity in two units is different to the same consumer and different consumers, we can say that producers have implemented price discrimination'.[5]

Summing up the above definitions, we can see that the basic meaning of price discrimination means that manufacturers ask the same or different consumers for different prices when selling different quantities of the same product, which does not include the difference in product prices caused by the difference in transportation costs, nor does it include the difference in price caused by the difference in quality. One thing we must emphasize is that if the difference in price reflects the difference in quality and cost of products, then the difference in price is not price discrimination. Therefore, there is not necessarily price discrimination when there

---

[3] Eatwell et al. [9].

[4] Kun [12].

[5] Taylor [22].

is price difference. Similarly, differentiated products cannot be completely equated with price discrimination.

In the physical market, the implementation of price discrimination must meet two basic conditions: (1) there is no possibility of arbitrage, that is, manufacturers can successfully separate the market, and consumers who buy goods at low prices can no longer sell them at high prices; (2) It is possible for manufacturers to obtain information about consumer demand functions, or to distinguish different types of consumers [24]. Similarly, in order to successfully implement price discrimination in the Internet market, Internet manufacturers must meet these conditions, but the ways and costs of meeting these conditions are different. For example, in the Internet market, vendors can obtain information about consumer needs through Java or 'click stream'.

4.2.2 The Form and Content of Price Discrimination in the Internet Market

4.2.2.1 The Basic Forms of Price Discrimination

British economist Pigou [18] divided price discrimination into three basic forms (Table 4.1):

From these three kinds of price discrimination, we can see that the second-level price discrimination is based on consumption motivation, the third-level price discrimination is based on consumption groups and the first-level price discrimination needs detailed information of users and the ability to price different users separately. The main difference between the second-level price discrimination and the third-level price discrimination is that the third-level price discrimination is based on the observable characteristics of different consumers, while the second-level price

Table 4.1 Types of price discrimination

Type	Content
First-degree price discrimination	When the seller charges a different price for each unit of product, and the price is exactly equal to the buyer's reservation price, the seller gets all the consumer surplus
Second-degree price discrimination	It means that the price depends on the purchase quantity, but does not depend on consumers. This pricing method is also called Nonlinrar Pricing method. At this time, every consumer is faced with the same price list, which stipulates different prices corresponding to different purchase quantities
Third-degree price discrimination	It means that different consumers pay different prices, but the price paid by the same consumer does not depend on the amount of purchases, as is the case when students enjoy half-price concessions by train

Source Collation of this study

discrimination cannot get direct information about consumers, and can only indirectly select consumers by providing price lists, so that consumers can buy automatically. First-class price discrimination means that individual pricing extracts all consumer surplus, but resale should be prevented.

4.2.2.2 The Form and Content of Price Discrimination

If the aforementioned three-level price discrimination is applied to Internet marketing, they can be expressed as [19]: (1) Personalized pricing: selling to each user at different prices. (2) Version division: Provide a product line, so that users can choose the most suitable version for themselves. (3) Group pricing: Set different prices for different groups of consumers, such as discounts on digital products for students.

Below, we respectively compare and analyze the performance and applicability of these three kinds of price discrimination in the physical market and the Internet market.

1. First-degree price discrimination—personalized pricing

First-degree price discrimination is also called complete price discrimination. As the modifier 'complete' shows, it is difficult to discriminate to this extent in the physical market or traditional market. There are many reasons why it is difficult to achieve complete price discrimination, but the most obvious reason is that it is extremely difficult to decide the maximum amount someone is willing to pay. And even if you know how much someone is willing to pay for your product, you can't offer the product to those who are unwilling to pay more while preventing those who are more willing to buy from taking advantage of this preferential condition. In e-commerce, sellers may eventually use first-class price discrimination to make each individual buyer pay the maximum price they are willing to pay. There are three factors that combine to determine the possibility of complete price discrimination: first, sellers can obtain detailed information about users' interests, such as: obtaining relevant information about consumers through billing and registering E-mail; Second, the product can be customized without adding extra cost; Third, users can pay their bills separately. In each of the above, the physical market is largely constrained by transaction costs including information costs, product change costs and complex payment costs. Because the Internet is more personal and interactive than catalogues, the implementation of total price discrimination by Internet vendors provides marketing opportunities that other media can't match. Cut-price sales, sell-offs and other forms of promotional pricing are effortless on the Internet, because prices can change instantaneously. These promotions can help you move products quickly, and they can also estimate the market's reaction to price changes.

Complete price discrimination requires detailed information of users and the ability to price different users separately. Although total price discrimination squeezes out all consumer surplus, it should also prevent resale. This possibility was previously considered only an academic issue, but with the emergence of electronic transactions, more detailed information about user information can be provided, which greatly reduces the biggest obstacle to the application of total price discrimination. Through price negotiations and auctions Internet, it is easier for sellers to price each person separately.

2. Second-degree price discrimination—versioning

Personalized pricing requires a certain understanding of consumers. This understanding often comes from consumers themselves, for example, when they put forward their own requirements and indicate the products they want to see or the types of information they are interested in. However, if there are no files provided by customers and no active participation of customers, we need to divide versions, that is, provide your information products to different market segments in different versions. In fact, in traditional marketing, publishers often design versions to emphasize customer differences. The key to their edition division of books is to postpone the publication of cheap editions. In this case, customers with high product evaluation have no patience to wait, while customers with low product evaluation are much easier to wait. After selling hardback copies to hardcore fans, libraries and book club, they introduced paperback copies so that all other fans could buy them.

Compared with the physical market, Internet marketing can use Internet technology for second-degree price discrimination. For example, Internet technology is used to partition versions closely related to delay. This strategy is to control the convenience of an information service by limiting its use time and place. For example, some Internet database providers provide a library license, which allows people who read in the library to use it without restrictions, while readers who are outside the library will be restricted when using it. It can also be versioned by the speed of operation, the flexibility of use and the integrity of functions. For example, when a software company sells software, it can use two versions, one low-priced but non-copyable version, and the other high-priced and non-write-protected version.

3. Three-degree price discrimination—group pricing

Compared with the physical market, it has more advantages to implement three-degree price discrimination in the Internet market. Specifically, it has the following three characteristics or forms: (1) utilizing the external effects of the Internet. In the Internet market, if the value of a product to a user depends on how many other members of the group to which it belongs use it, it is very possible to use it for three-degree price discrimination by setting a product as the standard. For example, Microsoft takes advantage of this desire for standardization in its Office components. (2) Make use of the lock-in effect of digital products. If an organization chooses a product as a standard, it will be very expensive to transfer because of the cost of coordination and retraining, and this time it can carry out three-degree price discrimination. Microsoft's operating system windows is an obvious example. (3) Make use of the sharing effect of digital products. In many cases, it is inconvenient for a single user to manage or organize all the information products they consume, and information intermediaries such as libraries and system administrators can accomplish this coordination. For example, Internet vendors can license sites, and they can also sell academic journals to libraries at high prices and individuals at low prices.

4.2.3 *Adverse Selection and the Obstacles and Reasons for the Implementation of Internet Price*

The characteristic of the Internet market is that you can search comprehensively, and you can search for information in large quantities and effectively with the help of search services. At the same time, because this kind of information search on the Internet is low cost and no cost, it also means relatively low transaction costs. The variability of digital products in electronic transactions and the accessibility of information to users can help Internet enterprises to make discriminatory pricing.

Although the Internet market has such marketing advantages, it does not mean that it has high market efficiency. One of the important reasons is the information asymmetry between buyers and sellers in the Internet market. Because of the asymmetry of information, the price discrimination strategy in Internet marketing may bring the following defects:

4.2.3.1 Users Will Lose the most Basic Price Control Ability

In the ideal differential pricing model, sellers may be effective for society by selling goods at the maximum price that users are willing to pay, but consumers are rarely willing to pay the highest price without complaining. What's more, the seller may decide to limit the quantity or refuse to sell by knowing the customer's information. In a sense, because of providing personal information to manufacturers, users will lose the most basic price control ability.

4.2.3.2 Price Discrimination Will Cause more Benefits to be Transferred from Buyers to Sellers

Vendors who know user information may price products according to the marginal valuation of each individual user rather than the marginal cost of the product. However, due to the virtual nature of the Internet, consumers should not only try to understand the quality distribution of products, but also understand the sales motivation of sellers. Because of the virtual nature of the Internet, it causes the information disadvantage of consumers and reduces the efficiency of transactions. In order to determine which option will bring greater benefits to users, it is necessary to have a complete understanding of the value of products that are suitable for users' needs. When the seller's evaluation of product quality is more subjective, it will aggravate the asymmetry of information. Generally speaking, price discrimination will lead to the transfer of benefits from buyers to sellers, and relatively speaking, users get less benefits than sellers.

4.2.3.3 The Adverse Selection Faced by Consumers Is more Serious

The 'quality-price' effect can be said to be an eternal topic in economics. At present, the marketing strategies such as price discrimination adopted in the Internet market can base the price of products on the evaluation of users and strive to reach the best point of price-quality, but because the most basic economic motivation of these marketing strategies is that manufacturers will virtually form a monopoly on products in order to reduce the competition between the same products and lock-in consumers, which will aggravate the information disadvantages faced by consumers on product quality.

In addition, the use of modern Internet technology for marketing, although it can be difficult to achieve in the traditional marketing or can not achieve the characteristics of Internet marketing price discrimination, but because this method will contain a strong subjective evaluation of product quality and quality preferences, products only choose different but not different quality, it will cause the same quality of products under the existence of huge price differences, which will exacerbate consumers to product quality information disadvantage, but also exacerbate the adverse selection faced by consumers. In this form of market conditions, users are forced to choose between buying products that meet their interests and paying at conservative prices, which is just more difficult for consumers.

4.2.4 The Ways to Avoid Adverse Selection in Internet Price Discrimination

It should be pointed out that we analyze the disadvantages of price discrimination in Internet marketing, not to put an end to it and cancel it. The reason lies in two aspects: On the one hand, it is indeed a price strategy that is easier to realize than in the traditional market; On the other hand, it is impossible to cancel it, because it is an inevitable means for the purpose of making profits in Internet distribution. Only by regulating price discrimination better can we give full play to its advantages and meet the needs of the market and consumers in the era of Internet economy.

From the strategic point of view, to carry out discriminatory pricing, on the one hand, it is necessary to make products differentiated by increasing the content of additional services, that is to say, it is best to combine with product differentiation, on the other hand, it is necessary to combine with product combination strategy. For example, in e-commerce, sellers may eventually use first-class price discrimination to make each individual buyer pay the maximum price they are willing to pay. In order to achieve complete price discrimination, sellers must be able to control consumer preferences in transactions, make separate payments and control user arbitrage. While carrying out discriminatory pricing, it is necessary to reduce users' resistance and prevent or minimize users' arbitrage.

To avoid the disadvantages caused by price discrimination in Internet marketing, we should resort to two main ways or methods:

4.2.4.1 The Reputation Channel

In the physical market, reputation plays a very important role in eliminating information asymmetry. Its essence lies in establishing mutual trust between the trading parties in the market to prevent or reduce the occurrence of 'dishonesty' (the specific analysis of Internet reputation will be carried out in Chapter 5). Good reputation management is conducive to the exertion of market functions, improving the efficiency of market transactions and increasing social welfare. Because of the virtual nature of the Internet and the late rise of e-commerce, there is no clear long-term profit motive to induce a large amount of funds to invest in reputation. Therefore, it may be more difficult for Internet product brands and company reputation to be the guarantee of product quality than in the physical market. But this does not mean that reputation signal will lose its position and function in the Internet market, on the contrary, we should make full use of it to strengthen the trust between buyers and sellers. To manage Internet reputation, we may pay more attention to the following issues:

1. To implement the strategy of reputation transfer (or brand extension), that is, to realize the reputation transfer from the physical market to the Internet market. In fact, many Internet companies are actually the same companies that already have a reputation in the physical market—they transfer their reputation to the electronic market. For example, Netscape was the first company to enter the web browser market. Before Microsoft entered the browser market, it occupied 80% of the market share. However, after Microsoft's Internet Explore browser came into the market, Microsoft took 20% of Netscape's market with its reputation advantage in the physical market in just one year. In addition, we can make up for the disadvantages of offline by combining Internet and offline.
2. Make full use of the advantages of Internet technology. Modern Internet technology has created unique conditions for us to establish Internet reputation, which traditional markets do not have. For example, three-dimensional animation and other advanced web design technology and forms of expression make the means of communication of Internet brand and reputation more powerful and visual impact, and greatly improve the efficiency of information dissemination.

4.2.4.2 Institutional Approaches

In order to avoid and reduce the vicious or unreasonable price discrimination in the Internet market, it is necessary to introduce non-economic methods such as government behavior or legal means.

1. Legal methods

In fact, in the physical market, the United States and other western countries have always studied and regulated some price discrimination that harms market competition as typical unfair competition behaviors. Among the legislation on price discrimination in various countries, the legislation of the United States is more perfect. In American legislation, Article 2 of Sherman Act deals with the use of predatory price discrimination to crowd out competitors and attempt to monopolize. Clayton Act focuses on different pricing between regions to weaken competition. Robinson-Patman Act most intensively and directly stipulates various price discrimination behaviors (this Act is also called Robinson-Patman Anti-Price Discrimination Act because it is specifically aimed at price discrimination), which is an amendment to Clayton Act.

In China, the Price Law also stipulates that operators who provide the same goods or services shall not discriminate against other operators with the same trading conditions.[6] However, it is worth noting that the price discrimination in the Price Law does not cover the price difference in the final consumption link, and the price receiver here only refers to the operator, not the consumer. What is more regrettable is that the relevant provisions are only for the price behavior in the physical market. Therefore, it is necessary for us to define the vicious price discrimination behavior in Internet trade and regulate it legally to protect the fundamental interests of consumers.

From the point of view of economics and law, the focus of economics on price discrimination is the impact of price discrimination on operators' profits and social welfare, while jurists and legislators generally pay attention to the damage of price discrimination to competition order and market environment. In fact, price discrimination is not completely anti-competitive, and price discrimination is ubiquitous in actual commercial activities. To some extent, it can be said that it is precisely because of the existence of price discrimination that the creativity of market subjects is activated and the benign development of market competition is promoted. Therefore, we must seek a balance between the two, of course, this is beyond the scope of this paper.

2. Legal use of privacy

To carry out price discrimination means to master the preference information of consumers, which means that sellers must know what each user wants, but this involves the personal privacy of consumers. Today, market research and research have

[6] Item 5 of Article 14 of the Price Law of the People's Republic of China (Chapter II Price Behavior of Operators), which came into effect on May 1, 1998, stipulates that 'providing the same goods or services and discriminating against other operators with the same trading conditions' is an unfair price behavior.

become an important part of product development and successful retail. As society moves from anonymous cash transactions to credit card payments and electronic payments, vendors find it much easier to gather information about users' behavior. However, with the development of Internet and digital software, privacy has become one of the biggest troubles brought by the Internet.

In essence, the right to privacy refers to the right not to be known by the public, free from publicity and unwarranted interference in private affairs unrelated to public affairs, such as personal living and activity space and all information about individuals. Specific to the right to privacy in the network, it mainly includes the right not to be peeped, invaded, interfered and illegally collected. Protecting the right to privacy has become an inevitable requirement for the stability of the whole society. Therefore, in order to avoid and reduce the problem of infringing on customers' privacy rights, it is necessary to carry out necessary norms. For example, the *AMA Code of Ethics for Marketing on the Internet* stipulates that information collected from consumers should be kept confidential and can only be used for clear purposes. This rule is concise and clear in all terms, and it is also used in the mechanism of collecting information on the Internet. In the spring of 2000, DoubleClick, an American online advertising company, collected and edited a large number of consumers' personal information on the largest scale, which attracted the attention of the media, the government and the public. The data direct control department of DoubleClick Company collects the data of offline consumers and makes a spreadsheet, which includes information such as name, address, personal purchase or home address. The most common way to get this kind of information is the use of cookies.[7] For another example, *the US Congress passed a Children's Online Privacy Protection Act* (COPPA).[8] The law stipulates that if websites or other media need to collect information from children aged 12 or younger, they must comply with the following rules: (1) Provide notification to parents; (2) Obtain the consent and confirmation of their parents before collecting, using or disclosing their information; (3) Allow parents to understand and correct one of the information; (4) Parents have the right to prohibit long-term use and collection of information; (5) Restrict the use of collected personal information to participate in children's games, as prizes, or other related activities; (6) Establish procedures to protect the confidentiality, security and uniform collection of personal information. In addition, the US Congress also requires FTC to implement some special rules to manage and enforce this bill.

---

[7] Cookies are text files stored on the client's (visitor's) hard disk (usually a user-built folder). The principle is that when a user browses a certain information on a certain web page for the first time, the cookie carried on the information will be automatically installed on your hard disk, and the cookie in the hard disk can send the information to the server that needs to collect this information. Internet companies use this method to track consumers' online location and personal information, and build their personal databases for better targeted purposes. cookies usually complete their information processing automatically without the user's knowledge, and this kind of tracking can present all the information of the user in all aspects. A Cookie includes the following five types of information: data string, expiration date, domain name, path and security status.

[8] Strauss and Frost [20].

Case: The failure of Amazon.com's price discrimination experiment[9]

The price discrimination experiment of Amazon.com, an e-commerce website in the United States, took place in 2000. It was the first large-scale price discrimination experiment in the history of e-commerce development, and ended in a fiasco in a short time.

Amazon officially opened in July 1995. Since the summer of 1996, the company has successfully implemented the affiliate marketing strategy. With the support of hundreds of thousands of affiliate websites, Amazon has rapidly emerged as the first brand in online sales in the United States. However, the operation of Amazon.com also exposed no small problems. Although Amazon's business is expanding rapidly, the loss amount is also increasing. In terms of business expansion, the website has also begun to encounter strong competition from some established portals, such as AOL and Yahoo. Under this background, Amazon urgently needs to realize profit, and the most reliable profit project is its longest-running books, music records and film and television discs. Because online sales do not increase the total demand for products in the market, Amazon started its famous price discrimination experiment in mid-September 2000 to improve the profit of its main products. As an emerging online retailer lacking industry background, Amazon does not have the excellent logistics capability of Barnes & Noble, nor has the access traffic as large as Yahoo and other portals. Amazon's most valuable asset is its 23 million registered users, and Amazon wants to realize as much profit as possible from these registered users. Amazon selected 68 kinds of DVD discs for a dynamic pricing experiment. In the experiment, Amazon determined the quotation level of these 68 kinds of discs based on the demographics of potential customers, shopping history at Amazon, online behavior and software systems used online. For example, a disc called Titus is quoted for $22.74 for new customers and $26.24 for old customers who show interest in the disc.

However, less than a month after the implementation of this price discrimination strategy, careful consumers discovered this secret. Through the communication in the music lover community called DVDTalk, hundreds of DVD consumers who paid high prices denounced Amazon's practice in fierce words on the Internet, and some even publicly stated that they would never buy anything in Amazon in the future. In addition, since Amazon recently announced that it tracks and records consumers' shopping habits and behaviors on the website, this incident has linked Amazon's price incident with sensitive online privacy issues.

In order to recover the increasingly prominent adverse effects, Amazon CEO Bezos had to personally apologize to consumers for this incident. Moreover, Amazon promised to give the largest discount to all consumers who bought these 68 DVDs during the price test. According to incomplete statistics, at least 6,896 customers who did not buy DVDs at the lowest discount price have already received the difference refunded by Amazon. At this point, Amazon's price test ended in complete failure.

---

[9] Part of this case comes from David (2000) and Liu [15].

Amazon has not only suffered economic losses, but its reputation has also been seriously damaged.

The failure of Amazon's price discrimination mainly lies in the fact that two basic conditions must be met for failure to realize price discrimination: (1) There is no possibility of arbitrage, that is, manufacturers can successfully separate the market, and consumers who buy goods at low prices can no longer sell at high prices; (2) It is possible for manufacturers to obtain information about consumer demand functions, or to distinguish different types of consumers. First of all, Amazon.com's pricing scheme tries to attract new customers by offering them more favorable prices, but it ignores one point: based on the customer data that Amazon.com already has, although it is difficult for new customers to pretend to be old customers, old customers can easily arbitrage by re-logging in and pretending to be new customers. As for the method of pricing according to the browser category used by customers, it also cannot prevent arbitrage, because Netscape browser and Microsoft's IE browser are basically available for free, and consumers who use Netscape browser can get lower quotations by using IE browser with little extra cost. Unable to stop arbitrage, Amazon.com's price discrimination strategy will not effectively improve the profit level in the long run. Secondly, Amazon.com uses customer shopping history, demographic data and other data in the process of price discrimination, but when collecting these data, it obtains customer consent under the guise of providing better personalized service to customers. Obviously, using these data for purposes that customers do not recognize is a typical moral hazard, which utilizes and aggravates customer adverse selection. In addition, there is a very important point, that is, Amazon's price discrimination scheme that discriminates against old customers deviates from the theory of relationship marketing. Amazon's sales mainly come from repeat purchases from regular customers, which accounted for 66% of total orders in the first quarter of 1999, and this proportion rose to 76% one year later. Amazon's strategy actually punishes the old customers who contribute the most to its profits, but it has no effective way to lock in the old customers, which will inevitably lead to the loss of old customers and the reduction of sales and profits.

4.3 Adverse Selection and Price Dispersion in Internet Market

4.3.1 The Price Dispersion Phenomenon in the Internet Market

Generally speaking, Price dispersion means that the same product has different prices. Compared with the traditional market, whether the network market has higher market efficiency has always been a topic that economists talk about. According to micro-information economics, with the decrease of search cost, the price dispersion should decrease (Stigler, 1961; MacMinn, 1980). Both theoretical and empirical analysis have proved that various search tools provided by the online market greatly reduce the cost of information search.[10] Therefore, some scholars believe that since the Internet greatly reduces the search cost, makes the industry value chain value-added, and shifts to the direction beneficial to consumers, so that consumers can obtain more product information, make it easier to compare prices, and the price dispersion should be lower, and the competition efficiency of the network market should be higher than that of the traditional market [2, 3].

However, relevant empirical studies do not consistently support this statement. Many scholars have made empirical comparative studies on online market and traditional market from two aspects of online price level and price dispersion, and obtained the opposite result: the price dispersion range of online products is larger than that of offline products, which is a persistent phenomenon and the most interesting phenomenon for economists.

Bailey [1] looked at the prices of books, CDs and software from 1996 to 1997. His research shows that online prices are higher than offline prices on average. He collected 24,000 price data about three commodities, and compared the differences between online and offline prices of the same commodity in absolute level, dispersion and frequency of change (menu cost). Bailey found that the online prices of the three commodities changed much more frequently, but the online prices were significantly higher than the offline prices. Prices in the online market for books and CDs are more discrete, while software is the opposite.

Brynjolfsson and Smith [5], building on Bailey's work, analyzed the characteristics of using the Internet as a sales channel (which mainly sells two similar but different products—books and CDs). They rely on econometrics to conclude that there are substantial and systematic differences in Internet retail prices. They found that the online prices of books and CDs changed more frequently and the price dispersion was greater. Among them, books account for 33% on average and CDs account for 25%.

In addition, Lee et al. [14] studied the online drug market in 1999–2000. The results show that the online price of over-the-counter drugs is lower than the offline price, but the complete price adjusted by distribution cost is higher than the offline price, the price dispersion is greater, and the price change is slower than that in the offline market.

The latest statistical research results have reached the same conclusion. Pan et al. [17] conducted 6739 price observations on 105 online retailers (involving 8 product categories and 581 items), and the results show that online price dispersion persists, even if the heterogeneity of retailers is excluded. Clemons et al. [8] used air ticket data provided by OTAs (online travel agents) to test price dispersion and product differences. They found that in many given OTAs, the same customer requirements will get different prices and special services. Although some changes are shown to be due to differences between different OTAs systems, such as reducing the number

---

[10] Economic analyses of relevant countries and international organizations (Zerdick et al., 2000; [7], policy reports [16, 23]; OECD 1999: Ch. 2) and market research (Alba et al., 1997) all suggest that Internet technology generally reduces search costs.

of lines and matching departure and return times, even if these factors are taken into account, the change range of fares still reaches 18% of the total OTAs, among which the difference of round-trip air tickets reaches 2.2%–28%. Su [21] analyzed the data of 14 product categories on the Internet, and found that there are 3 types of products (books, CDs and airline tickets) whose price changes are the biggest, and the CD market is the biggest price dispersion.

Obviously, the existing results are inconsistent with the theoretical logic of traditional economics. Although some studies have found that online price level is lower than offline price level, and some studies have found that online price level is higher than offline price level, all studies have found that the price dispersion in online market is greater. Therefore, this produces a 'price paradox' which contradicts the traditional economic theory.

4.4 Adverse Selection and Price Dispersion in the Internet

Different scholars have provided various reasons for the price dispersion.

According to Brynjolfsson and Smith [5], offline price dispersion comes from two different heterogeneity of retailers: heterogeneity of consumer perception, heterogeneity of retailer brand and trust. They believe that these differences may be magnified among online sellers compared with traditional business channels.

Bailey [1] attributed his observation of higher price levels in the Internet market to immaturity. This explanation can be confirmed by Brynjolfsson and Smith's conclusion, because the latter's research data was collected two years later than the former. In the meantime, the online book and CD market should become more mature, so its price level will be lower.

Chen and Hitt [6] attributed the price discrepancy to the difference of customer loyalty to the brand.

Lal and Sarvary [13] attributed the price dispersion to the difference of 'Digital Attributes' of products. Generally speaking, digital attributes are those product attributes that are mainly evaluated by visual inspection and can be transmitted by the Internet; Non-digital attributes are those that can only be evaluated by physical inspection of products and cannot be transmitted through the Internet. They believe that when there are enough network users and non-digital attributes are not particularly important, consumers will more identify with their familiar brands, which will lead to price dispersion due to price monopoly.

Clemons et al. [8] think that because customers need to 'register' to obtain the information they need, so as to reduce the time of personal search and obtain the qualification of booking tickets, when the transfer cost and search cost are 'non-zero', the chances of customers choosing in OTAs will be reduced.

Su [21] pointed out that there are two factors related to the price dispersion in the online market, that is, the inducement of online retailers' customer search and the evaluation of commodity utility.

Summing up the previous scholars' views, they actually attribute the reasons of price dispersion to the following aspects: (1) the differences in network market signals, such as trademarks and brands; (2) Consumers' cognition and loyalty to products; (3) Consumers' position in the market and their 'path dependence' on network tools, such as the size of transfer costs; (4) Digital/non-digital attributes of products; (5) Marketing strategies of online manufacturers, such as product induction. The reasons listed by the above scholars all explain the phenomenon of network price dispersion to a certain extent, but I think the fundamental reason for price dispersion is the 'lemon' problem existing in the network market.

As we pointed out in the previous section when we discussed online price discrimination, the online environment enables enterprises to easily collect information on consumer preferences, providing conditions for online enterprises to implement discriminatory pricing. The extremely low menu cost and customization cost enable online enterprises to use the interface to influence the information that consumers with different preferences can get, and further divide consumers, thus realizing the powerful price discrimination ability of online enterprises.

On the other hand, due to strategic considerations, the seller did not provide relevant comprehensive information. In fact, the information provided by suppliers is to pursue differentiation strategy—it prevents the possibility of comparing bids, and some information cannot and will not be verified [7]. Moreover, even if information is provided, this method will contain strong subjective evaluation and quality preference of the seller for product quality. It is obviously impossible for consumers to try to understand not only the quality distribution of products but also the sales motivation of sellers when they want to buy products. This situation aggravates the information disadvantage faced by consumers on product quality, aggravates the adverse selection faced by consumers and causes the price difference of products with the same quality, resulting in price dispersion.

From the consumer's point of view, although in the network market environment, they can use various Internet search and comparison tools to obtain more product information such as price with lower search cost. But the Internet reduces the search cost of consumers, but also reduces the search cost of enterprises. It has a dual function. For example, 'Shopbots'[11], which currently exists on the Internet, improves the price elasticity of demand, but someone invented 'Pircebots', which is a price algorithm in response to the inquiry of 'Shopbots' (Greenwald and Kephart 1999), thus forming an interaction between 'Shopbots' consumers and 'Pircebots' suppliers on the Internet. In addition, Gallaughe and Downing [10] found that the information obtained through search engines (such as Google) and price comparison sites (such as Pricescan.com) is incomplete. The reason for this phenomenon, Choi et al. [7] once on the Internet search engine insufficiency boils down to the following four points: (1) The complete including all websites and all documents directory does not exist.

[11] ShopBot is a price comparison agent system, which extracts information from online sellers' websites. The algorithm is mainly aimed at the pages that provide queries in the form of forms, and the returned search results are product information pages displayed in the form of tables. The technique of extracting information from the results page combines heuristic search, pattern matching and inductive learning.

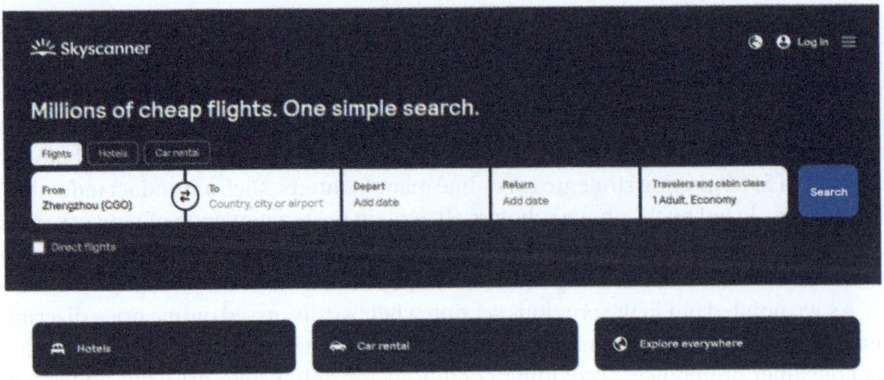

Fig. 4.3 Page of price comparison website Skyscanner.com

The reason is that in order to make up for the loss caused by compiling databases, many search engines only focus on attracting advertisers instead of improving the integrity of data and search efficiency; (2) Because the website is constantly updated, the database is also inaccurate and outdated, and they will often give users some links that no longer exist; (3) Because the digital document metadata standard has not been established, some websites will bring information irrelevant to search keywords; (4) Some search engine information is selected on vague criteria, which affects the objectivity of the results. For example, some search engines ignore websites that are considered offensive、indecent and frivolous according to their own standards.

In this case, only network consumers with sufficient information may buy products with low prices, while network consumers without sufficient information may adopt random purchase methods, and they may buy products with high prices. On the other hand, if a consumer is still in adverse selection with the help of search engines and price comparison tools, he can only use reputation, brand and other means to avoid adverse selection—which often requires consumers to pay 'reputation rent' besides price (we will analyze this issue in detail in Chapter 5).

At present, the appearance, existence and development of 'comparative shopping' website shows the fact that the price dispersion exists and lasts in the network market from the opposite side. The so-called form of 'comparative shopping', in short, is to let netizens search for a certain commodity on the Internet and obtain information about the commodity in many online stores, among which price is one of the contents to be compared. In the United States, the more representative websites are Skyscanner.[12] Skyscanner is a travel search platform that offers instant online comparisons of millions of routes from over a thousand airlines as well as car rentals and hotels (see Fig. 4.3).

In addition, the emergence and development of price comparison websites not only explain the fact of network price dispersion, but also provide us with a means to reduce network adverse selection. Therefore, good price comparison websites,

12 https://www.skyscanner.com/

such as Pricescan, have unlimited marketing influence. Heavyweight search engines Google and Yahoo have also launched comparative shopping services to gain more business opportunities.

4.4.1 Conclusion

Market efficiency is the foundation of market existence, and it has always been the focus of economists' attention. Bertrand's price competition model (1883) describes the price competition behavior of firms in a market where there is no difference in products, consumers have complete information and search costs are zero, in which all firms price according to marginal costs. However, Bertrand model is only a theoretical model, and the real market certainly cannot satisfy the above assumptions, especially the network market. The previous analysis shows that the intrinsic reason for the price dispersion of network products lies in the asymmetry of quality information and the adverse selection existing in the network market. Therefore, in order to reduce the price dispersion and improve the transaction efficiency, it is necessary to explore the methods to solve the adverse selection problem in the network market.

References

1. Alba, Joseph, John Lynch, Barton Weitz, Chris Janiszewski, Richard Lutz, Alan Sawyer, Stacy Wood (1997) Interactive home shopping: incentives for consumers, retailers, and manufacturers to participate in electronic marketplaces. J. Marketing 61 (July) 38–53
2. Zerdick A, Picot A, Schrape K, Artope A, Goldhammer K, Lange UT, Vierkant E, Lopez-Escobar E, Silverstone R (2000) Strategies for the Digital Marketplace, Springer
3. Bailey JP (1998) Electronic commerce: prices and consumer issues for three products: books, compact discs, and software. Working paper OCDE/GD(98)4, Organization for Economic Co-Operation and Development [Online]. http://www.oecd.org/dsti/sti/it/ec/prod/ie98-4.pdf
4. Bakos JY (1991) A strategic analysis of electronic marketplaces. MIS Quart 15(3):295–310
5. Benjamin R, Wigand R (1995) Electronic markets and virtual value chains on the information superhighway. Sloan Management Rev (Winter):62–72
6. Bin Z (2000) Priceine.com, a network enterprise, and its consumer pricing marketing model. Jiangsu Bus Theory 6:28–30
7. Brynjolfsson E, Smith M (2000) Frictionless commerce? A comparison of internet and conventional retailers. Manage Sci 46:563–585
8. Chen P, Hitt LM (2000) Switching cost and brand loyalty in electronic markets: evidence from on-line retail brokers. 21st Annual International Conference on Information Systems, Brisbane
9. Choi SY, Stahl DO, Whinston AB (1997) The economics of electronic commerce. Macmillan Technical Publishing, Indianapolis
10. Clemons EK, Hann IH, Hitt LM (2002) Price dispersion and differentiation in online travel: an empirical investigation. Manage Sci 48(4):534–549
11. Eatwell J, Milgate M, Newman P (1987) The new Palgrave dictionary of economics, The Macmillan Press
12. Gallaughe J, Downing C (1999) Market leadership and the web portal industry: an emperical investigation. Working Paper, Boston College

13. Greenwald AR, Kephart JO (1999) Shopbots and pricebots. Proceedings of Sixteenth International Joint Conference on Artificial Intelligence
14. Kun M (2001) Principles of economics, translated by Xiaomin Liang. Peking University Press, Beijing
15. Lal R, Sarvary M (1999) When and how is the internet likely to decrease price competition? Mark Sci 18(4):485–504
16. Lee J, Jinwoo K, Jae YM (2000) What makes Internet users visit cyber stores again? Key design factors for customer loyalty. Proceedings of the CHI 2000 Conference on Human Factors in Computing Systems, 305–312
17. Liu X (2003) A case study of differential pricing strategy in internet marketing. Price Theory Practice 7:59–60
18. MacMinn, RD (1980) Search and Market Equilibrium, Journal of Political Economy 88:308–327
19. Organization for Economic Cooperation and Development (1997) Knowledge-based economy. Machinery Industry Press, Beijing
20. Pan X, Ratchford B, Shankar V (2002) Can price dispersion in online markets be explained by differences in e-tailer service quality? J Acad Market Sci 30(4):433–446
21. Pigou AC (1920) The economic of welfare. Macmillan, London
22. Shapiro C, Varian H, Rules I (2000) Strategic guidance of network economy. Renmin University of China Press, Beijing
23. Stigler, (1961) GJ The economics of information. Journal of political economy 69(3):213–225
24. Strauss J, Frost R (2001) E-marketing, 2nd edn. New Jersey: Prentice-Hall, p 416
25. Su BC (2003) Economic and empirical analysis of consumer purchase intentions in electronic and traditional retail channels, Internet retailer pricing strategies, and price dispersion on the Internet. Dissertation (PhD), The University of Connecticut
26. Taylor F (1997) Theory of industrial organization. Renmin University of China Press, Beijing
27. US Department of Commerce (1999) The emerging internet economy II. Secretariat on Electronic Commerce, US Department of Commerce, Washington, DC. http://www.ecommerce.gov/
28. Zhang W (2001) Introduction to Stiglitz. Renmin University of China Press, Beijing

Chapter 5
Adverse Selection and Reputation Operation Mode of the Internet Market

As mentioned earlier, reputation, as a solution to adverse selection, plays an important role not only in the physical market, but also in the network market. In this chapter, we will analyze the role and operation mechanism of reputation in solving network adverse selection.

5.1 Reputation and the 'Lemon' Problem in the Internet Market

5.1.1 The Definition of Reputation

There are many different definitions and understandings of reputation. Levitt [1] believes that reputation comes from consumers' cognition, which is composed of the popularity, good or bad, reliability, reputation or trustworthiness of an enterprise. Spence [2] argues that reputation is the result of a competitive process, in which he points out that firms send signals to the public about their main traits in order to gain maximum social status. According to Herbig and Milewicz [3], reputation is a long-term and consistent evaluation of an individual's characteristics, which is based on the individual's willingness and ability to repeatedly perform certain actions in similar activities. Some scholars believe that reputation refers to a kind of social memory composed of many factors, such as past experience, products produced in the past, management performance, etc. It is the value judgment made by the general public for various characteristics of an enterprise [4].

From the marketing point of view, reputation has long been regarded as the key factor of successful marketing. Davidson [5] argues that reputation can help win public attitudes. When reputable businesses are affected by negative news, consumers are more likely to correct, filter or even eliminate their feelings. Fombrun and Van

Y. Pan, *Trust Management in the Chinese E-Commerce Market*,
Advanced Studies in E-Commerce, https://doi.org/10.1007/978-981-97-1115-4_5

Table 5.1 Definition of reputation in various academic documents

Discipline	Definition of reputation
Accounting	Reputation is regarded as an intangible asset and will or should be endowed with financial value
Economics	Reputation is regarded as a signal
Marketing	Whether it is promising from the perspective of customers or end users, and focus on the methods and means needed to form reputation
Organizational behavior	It is regarded as a sensory experience of employees, or the cognition of an organization owned by people with interests within an organization
Sociology	It can be regarded as an overall evaluation of a company's performance, which is related to the expectations and benchmarks behind it
Decision science	Obstacles that are regarded as assets and motives. Because reputation is based on cognition, it is difficult to manage

Source Fombrun and Van Riel [6]

Riel [6] have summarized definitions of reputation in different academic fields, as shown in Table 5.1.

No matter how we define reputation, it is certain that corporate reputation is the degree to which an enterprise gains public trust. Its essence lies in the establishment of mutual trust between the trading parties in the market, so as to prevent or reduce the occurrence of 'dishonesty'. As a means to solve adverse selection, reputation is a very strong market signal. This chapter analyzes and discusses the operation law of network reputation on this basis.

Next, we start our analysis with the relationship between adverse selection and reputation.

5.2 Reputation and Network Adverse Selection

According to the previous discussion, in addition to non-economic means, the methods to solve the network 'lemon' problem can be roughly divided into three ways: one way is to expose information to the counterparty so that the other party can distinguish between advantages and disadvantages, such as signal signaling; another way is to identify the information released by the other party or the quality itself, such as searching; the third way is to arbitrate the product quality through a third party, such as the method of network quality intermediary. In fact, these three ways have an inevitable relationship with reputation: the method of exposing information to the counterparty is actually the process of establishing reputation, and the enterprise tells consumers that its products are high-quality products rather than inferior products through brand, which is often successful; the process of network search is actually the process of consumers speculating and screening the reputation of products or manufacturers; when consumers use intermediaries, they must also consider the reputation of intermediaries, and intermediaries may pay more attention to their own reputation, otherwise they will lose their own market.

Therefore, reputation plays a very important role in eliminating information asymmetry. A good corporate reputation will help to improve the expectations of buyers for the quality of products provided by enterprises. Therefore, when consumers want to buy a product without knowing the quality of the product and face adverse selection, corporate reputation becomes one of the important evaluation indexes of consumers' purchasing decision, because corporate reputation can be used to ensure the quality of the product in the market.

We can use the Akerlof model of Swarm platform to illustrate the role of reputation mechanism in solving adverse selection and improving market transaction efficiency [7]. If we use reputation transmission as a feedback mechanism, we can establish an Akerlof simulation environment with multiple agents. The running results of the model are shown in Figs. 5.1 and 5.2. Among them, M1 indicates the market with high integrity (reasonable pricing accounts for the majority), and the corresponding indicators are indicated by blue line (deep); M2 indicates the market with low integrity (unreasonable pricing accounts for the majority), and the corresponding index is indicated by yellow line (shallow).

We can see from the figure that: (1) the quality of cars traded in the market M1 with higher integrity is higher than that in the market M2 with lower integrity; (2) The market M1 with higher integrity is higher than the market M2 with lower recognition in terms of transaction quantity and growth rate of transaction quantity, and the transaction activity is higher (see Fig. 5.1, the growth rate of transaction quantity is expressed by the slope of the curve).

The above operation results show that in the market with high integrity, it can achieve high efficiency in average transaction quality, market transaction activity and other aspects; the market with strong fraud is just the opposite. This can be identified as some kind of 'word of mouth' or 'brand effect'. Therefore, it shows that although adverse selection exists, under the influence of brand effect and feedback

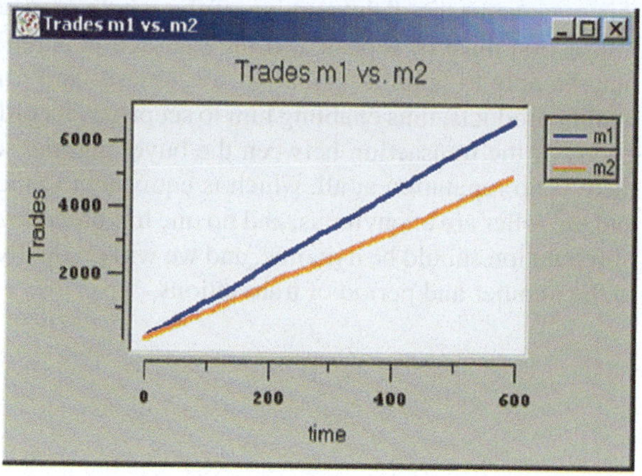

Fig. 5.1 Transaction quantity comparison figure

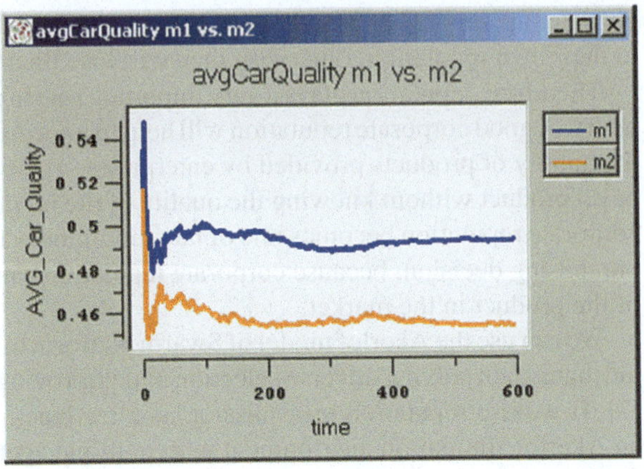

Fig. 5.2 Average quality comparison chart

mechanism, the transaction efficiency of markets with higher integrity will be higher than that of markets with lower integrity.

Below, we establish a reputation model to analyze the internal mechanism of reputation operation, so as to provide a theoretical thinking for reputation management.

5.3 The Reputation Model Based on the 'Lemon' Problem

5.3.1 The Premise of Building a Reputation Model

Obviously, reputation can only be established in the process of repeating the trading behaviors of market participants. The 'lemon' principle or Akerlof model tells us that because consumers can't judge the quality of products when purchasing products, this may cause the disintegration of the whole market. To break this deadlock, the transaction must be repeated. If the transaction is repeated in the market, the seller may be able to build a reputation for honesty and trustworthiness by selling good quality products, thus enabling him to set prices according to the actual quality of the goods. If the transaction between the buyer and the seller is only carried out once, there is no reputation at all, which is equivalent to the situation that both the buyer and the seller are anonymous, and no one has brand awareness. Therefore, the model of reputation should be dynamic, and we will gradually develop the model according to the number and period of transactions.

5.3.2 *The Construction of Reputation Model*

5.3.2.1 Reputation Investment Period

Assuming that manufacturers producing similar products are divided into manufacturer 1 and manufacturer 2, in which manufacturer 1 produces high-quality products and manufacturer 2 produces inferior products, that is, 'lemon' products, their unit production costs are c_1 and c_2 respectively, and $c_1 > c_2 > 0$, that is, the cost of high-quality products should be higher than that of 'lemon' products. For the sake of analysis, we assume that the product consumed by consumers is a unit, at the same time, we assume that the price of the product is *p*, and the consumer evaluates the quality of the product as *q*. We also assume that the utility function obtained by consumers is $U_B = nq - p$, where n represents the consumer's purchase variable, $n = 1$ represents the purchase of high-quality products, and $n = 0$ represents the purchase of 'lemon' products. In this case, the utility of vendor 1 is $U_1 = p - c_1$, and the utility of vendor 2 is $U_2 = p - c_2$. Obviously, $U_1 < U_2$. The utility that consumers get when they buy high quality products is *q-p*, and the utility that consumers get when they buy 'lemon' products is $-p$. If the transaction occurs, we can get two situations: (1) If the product purchased by consumers is a high-quality product, the social welfare is $\pi_S = (p - c_1) + (q - p) = q - c_1$. It can be seen from the formula that as long as $q > c_1$, the production of high-quality products creates social welfare. (2) If the product purchased by consumers is 'lemon', that is, inferior products, the social welfare is $\pi_S = (p - c_1) + (-p) = -c_1 < 0$. It can be seen from the formula that the production of inferior products is harmful to social welfare in this case.

If the transaction relationship is repeated and continuous, consumers who buy high-quality products in the first phase will still go to the original factory to buy them in the second phase. Consumers who buy inferior products in the first phase will not go to the original manufacturers to buy products. However, in this period, the income of Firm 1 is lower than that of Firm 2, and even adopts the strategy of low price to attract consumers, so that it will bear the net loss. Therefore, the first period should be the period when manufacturers make net investment in reputation.

5.3.2.2 A Limited Number of Repeated Transactions

Now, let's analyze what vendor 1 needs to maintain its reputation.

Assuming that firm 1 produces and sells good quality products for the t th time, and assuming that the time discount factor or discount factor is δ^1, the current value obtained after a finite number of transactions is:

$$(p - c_1) + \delta(p - c_1) + \delta^2(p - c_1) + \ldots + \delta^{t-1}(p - c_1) = \frac{1 - \delta^t}{1 - \delta}(p - c_1) \tag{5.1}$$

If Firm 1 changes to produce inferior products, it will get a profit of $p - c_2$ in the current period. Therefore, in order for Firm 1 to be willing to invest in reputation, it should have:

$$\frac{1-\delta^t}{1-\delta}(p-c_1) > (p-c_2) \tag{5.2}$$

It can be seen from this illustration that in order for Manufacturer 1 to continue to maintain its reputation without producing inferior products, the values of t and δ, that is, the production time, must meet the conditions of Eq. (5.2). However, if Manufacturer 1 considers its own profit, it may also produce inferior products to reduce costs. In this case, even if firm 1 can meet the requirements of (5.2) in period $t-1$ and changes to produce 'lemon' products after period t, consumers will identify firm 1 as a manufacturer of inferior products and stop buying its products, and the reputation of the firm may be destroyed. Therefore, no matter how many times the transaction is carried out, as long as the last transaction is 'lemon' products, the reputation of the manufacturer will not be established.

5.3.2.3 Unlimited Repeated Transactions

What we are considering above is a finite number of repetitions. If the transaction is an infinite number of repetitions, this problem can be solved. If we look at the number of transactions as endless, then (5.1) becomes:

$$(p-c_1)+\delta(p-c_1)+\delta^2(p-c_1)+\ \ldots\ +\delta^{t-1}(p-c_1)+\cdots=\frac{1}{1-\delta}(p-c_1) \tag{5.3}$$

And (5.2) becomes:

$$\frac{1}{1-\delta}(p-c_1) > p-c_2 \tag{5.4}$$

By sorting out formula (5.4), we can get:

$$p > c_1 + \left(\frac{1}{\delta}-1\right)(c_1-c_2) \tag{5.5}$$

$$\delta > \frac{c_1-c_2}{p-c_2} \tag{5.6}$$

Equation (5.5) not only expresses to us the 'separation equilibrium' condition that distinguishes high-quality products from 'lemon' products, but also expresses to us the 'reputation rent' obtained after realizing this 'separation equilibrium'.

It can be seen from (5.6) that this 'separation equilibrium' can be achieved as long as δ is large enough.

5.3.3 Conclusion

Through the derivation and analysis of the reputation model, we can get the following conclusions:

[Conclusion 1] From the derivation and analysis of the model, we can see that reputation management is actually a management process of 'reputation chain'. When one part of the 'reputation chain' goes wrong, its reputation will be lost.

[Conclusion 2] Enterprises or products need to have enough patience to establish reputation. This conclusion can be seen from (5.6), that is, δ is large enough. It tells us that a good reputation must be created through long-term and accumulated efforts. Ensuring that operators have long-term expectations is the foundation of sound development of reputation, not only because operators' reputation can be established and formed only in long-term management practice, but also because only operators who have long-term expectations for the future will pay attention to their own reputation in management activities. As long as the operator expects that the 'game' can be repeated, the operator will overcome the tendency of 'opportunism' behavior; on the contrary, if the operator expects a one-time 'game' relationship, it is possible to attach importance to the current income and have 'opportunistic' behavior.

[Conclusion 3] Products or enterprises with reputation should get a certain 'reputation rent'. Equation (5.5) not only expresses to us the 'separation equilibrium' condition that distinguishes high-quality products from 'lemon' products, but also expresses to us the 'reputation rent' obtained after realizing this 'separation equilibrium'. Among them, the part $(\frac{1}{\delta} - 1)(c_1 - c_2)$ higher than the cost c_1 in formula (5.5) is the 'reputation rent' of the manufacturer, which is the enjoyment it should get by virtue of its reputation. 'Reputation rent' is the incentive to gain and maintain reputation, and it is also the condition of 'separation and equilibrium' to distinguish its products from 'lemon' products.

[Conclusion 4] Reputation management needs certain institutional guarantee to play its role. Its purpose is to ensure that the 'reputation chain' can continue to occur and repeat the game behavior. This system is not simply equivalent to the national judicial system, but should be a system between self-enforcing reputation and the national judicial system, such as credit rationing system in capital market and certification system in labor market.

[Conclusion 5] Reputation is a kind of capital. The management process of reputation should include investment period and enjoyment period. Enterprises must invest in reputation, which is a necessary condition for creating a good reputation of enterprises.

5.4 The Characteristics of Adverse Selection and Reputation Management in the Internet Market

It should be emphasized that reputation method, as the main way to solve adverse selection in the market, is still a very important method in the network market, but its expression and utilization will be different from those in the traditional market. To manage online reputation, it is necessary to strengthen the role of online reputation in solving adverse selection according to the particularity of online market. Applying the model and conclusion established in the previous section to network reputation management, using network reputation to solve adverse selection in network market, it should have the following characteristics:

5.4.1 Fully Understand the Characteristics of Network Reputation

As mentioned above, in the network market, the role of reputation in solving adverse selection will encounter new difficulties, which are mainly manifested in the difficulty of identifying the identity of network manufacturers, the subjectivity of network product quality evaluation and the diversity of network producers. Because network products are mostly manufactured and sold by virtual people on the Internet, and each user is a producer and potential seller, the traditional way of reputation building may not work well in the network market. In addition, although the entry of the network market has a low entry barrier, because the reputation of manufacturers is based on the repeated purchases of consumers, even reputable companies hardly have much advantage when consumers do not repeat purchases. Therefore, it may be more difficult for online product brand and company reputation to guarantee product quality than in the physical market.

Although it is more difficult to establish one's own reputation in the network market than in the traditional market, this does not mean that it is impossible to establish the reputation of enterprises or products in the Internet market. In order to establish reputation through signals in the network market, network manufacturers have to spend more costs. Usually, they must bear the losses suffered at the initial stage of entering the market and provide information products free of charge or at a low price—because before they establish reputation, even if their information products are of high quality, they cannot ask for high prices for their products. This means that the critical point that network vendors can bear may be the huge sunk cost. Manufacturers who want to enter the Internet market should have a clear understanding of this point.

5.4.2 *Implement the Strategy of 'Reputation Transfer', That is, to Realize the Reputation Transfer From the Physical Market to the Network Market*

In fact, many online companies are actually the same companies that already have a certain reputation in the physical market—they transfer their reputation in the physical market to the electronic market. For example, Microsoft (http://www.microsoft.com) and IBM (http://www.ibm.com) have tried to use their reputation and brand in the physical market as a stepping stone to enter e-commerce, which provides certain advantages for new companies entering e-commerce. If successful, this will pose a certain threat to existing companies in the new market. However, this reputation transfer, in terms of product quality and service, needs to be recognized by customers in new markets. In this way, in the electronic market, if the quality of products is difficult to guarantee, the life of this reputation transfer will be very short.

5.4.3 *Recognize Your Own 'Reputation Chain'*

This reputation chain is reflected not only in the transaction, but also before and after the transaction, both in the Internet market and in the physical market. To some extent, the role of word-of-mouth in the physical market is more important than that in the online market. Although an enterprise can repair a damaged reputation, it will never be repaired to its previous undamaged state, and its reputation property will depreciate rapidly. On the contrary, if enterprises are good at reputation management, the value of reputation property will increase day by day with the expansion of 'reputation chain', and many potential values will be created.

5.4.4 *Make Full Use of the Advantages of Network Technology*

Modern network technology has created unique conditions for us to establish network reputation, which traditional markets do not have. From the current situation, there are some methods as follows:

5.4.4.1 Free Online Products

Free-products online is especially suitable for software developers who want to build their reputation online. Free software, trial software is provided free of charge by software developers. Beta software is software that customers who like the product

Fig. 5.3 Free and trial software available on freewarehome.com

try for free at a certain time before they decide to buy it, while commercial software always provides users with demonstration versions of key parts for free. The freewarehome site, for example, has a large collection of free software (Fig. 5.3).

The quality of digital products, such as software, can only be known through use. General customers are unwilling to use products that do not know the quality. Through trial, customers have an understanding of the quality and usefulness of products, and thus manufacturers have established the reputation of products and enterprises. Of course, strictly speaking, a trial product is not equal to a free product. The characteristic of a trial product is that it will be paid for when it is used after the trial period has passed. For example, the American Association of Software Professionals (ASP) defines trial software as: 'It is a marketing method rather than software. It does not pay first like the usual sales channel, but makes you try it for a period of time before buying'. Therefore, it can be said that the benefit of trial software lies in making consumers realize the quality of products, and it also encourages manufacturers to produce high-quality products.

5.4.4.2 Bundled Sales

Using bundling is also a better method, because it can not only save consumers' search costs, but also enable high-quality sellers to attract customers with low enough prices and signal effects produced by the high quality of products in the past. The most obvious example of bundling in the software industry is Microsoft Office, a product bundled with a word processor, a spreadsheet, a database and a presentation tool. These products can also be provided separately, which is the difference between bundling and Tying. Network technology provides technical support for customized bundled sales of digital products. Online customers can freely choose combinations in the database of digital products and make customized bundled purchases. For example, the publishers of Personal Journal and The Wall Street Journal, founded by Dow Jones & Company, Inc., send electronic magazines to subscribers, and at the same time, any news or articles related to these companies and stock information will be bundled and sent to subscribers. Of course, consumers are also facing a lock-in situation under this sales model.

5.4.4.3 Attention Selling

In the era of information explosion, the phenomenon of information overload is very serious, in which case attention becomes a scarce resource. Because the quality of attention can be calculated by counting 'click-through rates' using current web technology, it can be sold as a product. Selling the audience's attention is an attractive way to support the provision of information. When a network vendor can provide high-quality information products, it is willing to pay a high price to attract attention first, so as to build credibility. In this sense, it is also a way to reduce the uncertainty of product quality.

5.4.4.4 Lease Credit

The so-called renting reputation means that manufacturers who have not yet established a reputation can use other people's reputation to sell their products. For example, many foreign automakers in the United States borrow American brands to sell their cars, so renting reputation is a marketing strategy for experienced products or when manufacturers have not yet established their own reputation. In the e-commerce market, because of the diversity and short lifetime of many products, especially digital products, rental reputation may be more usable.

5.4.4.5 Web Design Techniques

Three-dimensional animation and other advanced web design technology and forms of expression, making the network brand and reputation communication means more powerful and visual impact, greatly improve the efficiency of information dissemination, it is conducive to the spread of reputation.

5.4.4.6 Co-branding

The birth of cobranding means that two different companies use their brands for the same product. This approach has special significance online because it is a good way for companies to work together through expertise and brand recognition. For example, Yahoo! First teamed up with TV Guide at Yahoo! The website publishes the TV program list. Since then, TV Guide has built its own brand for its website, while Yahoo! Then realized brand alliance with Gist and published TV programs. For example, EarthLink, the largest independent Internet service provider in the United States, joined forces with Sprint Telephone Company in early 1998 and signed a long-term contract. The two companies launched a co-branding business, naming it EarthLink-Sprint and designing the logo. They use co-branding to provide ISP services to Sprint customers and win over AOL customers.[1]

Case: The reputation and brand development track of JCPenney in the United States[2]

JCPenney is listed by the National Retail Organization as the leader in online sales and the most popular retail website for consumers. We can find the relationship between the rapid development of online retailing and corporate reputation from the company's development history.

JCPenney.com was founded by James Cash Penney in Wyoming in 1902, selling fabrics and clothing. By 1913, JCPenney Company was established, and at that time it had 36 branches. In 1927, there were 892 stores with sales of US $150 million, which was the largest chain of stores at that time. At present, it has 270,000 employees, and its target consumers are middle-class consumers in the United States. The company consists of three parts: (1) physical stores. It has 1100 domestic stores in the United States and branches in Brazil, Mexico and other places. (2) Direct selling companies. Composed of catalogs and online retail stores, it is the largest consumer catalogue company in the United States. (3) Eckerd Pharmacy consists of 2650 pharmacies. In 1962, the company acquired General Commodities Company, which operates catalogue business. In 1963, the company started catalogue business. By 1993, it had established six distribution centers and became the largest catalogue retail company in the United States. In 1994, the company established its first website to cooperate with the directory telephone ordering business. In 1995, the website began to accept online orders, and in 1996, the company selectively sold catalog products online. In 1998, the company invested 2.2 billion US dollars to establish online retail channels. In 1999, all catalog products were presented online, and online sales increased dramatically. The retail sales of the whole catalog and online retail companies reached 4 billion US dollars (Fig. 5.4).

The first reason why JCPenney has achieved such great achievements is that JCPenney's reputation and brand have been extended in the online sales market. JCPenney's traditional retail stores have inherent advantages in developing online retailing. That is, before the company sold online, it already had a huge catalog consumer group (JCPenney Catalog), which is a major foundation for the success of the company's online retail, and it has great reputation communication power and radiation power. Catalog retail is before the emergence of online sales, consumers through the company directory, telephone or mail to the company orders, through

[1] Source: http://www.spiderline.com/.

[2] Information on the case is available on the company's website (http://www.jcpenney.net/), Blakey [8] and Cheng Hua [9].

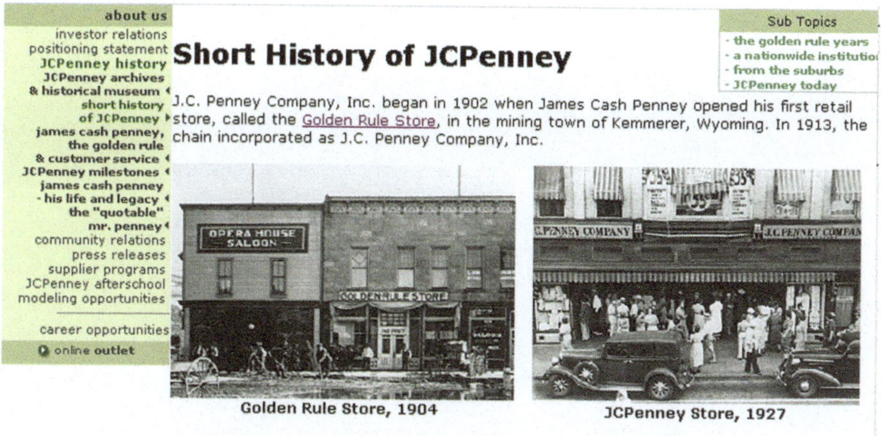

Fig. 5.4 JCPenney's web page about the history of the company

the mail to get goods. When JCPenney switched catalog consumers from catalog shopping to online shopping, consumers' existing shopping experience, trust in the quality of the company's products and good compatibility can quickly adapt to the gradually innovative online retail model. Although online shopping consumers can't touch goods, and there is a certain quality uncertainty, that is, 'lemon' problem, under the strong reputation and brand support of the company, adverse selection in the transaction process can be reduced. Compared with pure network companies, consumers are more likely to accept and trust the company. This is the secret that the traditional retailers of the company have developed online retailing faster in recent years.

References

1. Levitt T (1965) Industrial purchasing behavior: a study of communications effects. Division of Research, Harvard Business School, Boston, MA
2. Spence AM (1974) Market signaling: informational transfer in hiring and related screening procedures. Harvard University Press, Cambridge, MA
3. Herbig P, Milewicz J (1995) To be or not to be...credible that is: a model of reputation and credibility among competing firms. Mark Intell Plan 13(6):24–33
4. Gray ER, John MT (1998) Balmer, managing image and corporate reputation. Long Range Plan 31(5):685–692
5. Davidson DK (1990) On corporate reputation: a reply to Dobson. Bus Soc 29(1):39–41
6. Fombrun C, Van Riel C (1997) The reputational landscape. Corp Reput Rev, vol 1 and 2
7. Ren B (2002) Complexity, models and economic research methods. Master Thesis of Renmin University of China
8. Blakey E (2000) Success story: JCPenney.com, E-Commerce Times
9. Cheng H (2002) Research on consumers' acceptance of online retailing mode. Econ Theory Econ Manag 7:62–65

References

Chapter 6
Adverse Selection and Operation Mode of the Internet Quality Intermediary

In traditional economics, market intermediary plays a very important role in solving adverse selection. Because of the existence of network 'lemon', in the network market where buyers and sellers can't fully solve the quality uncertainty, the market mechanism based on intermediary can be more effective than the market mechanism without intermediary or rule system. However, because the 'lemon' problem in the network market and the 'lemon' problem in the traditional market have different characteristics and manifestations, it also determines that the intermediary in the network market will have different means to solve the information asymmetry. So, what is the role of e-commerce market intermediary? In fact, the network intermediary provides product quality information as a third party, which can eliminate the possibility of market failure due to quality uncertainty. This chapter will analyze this problem. From the perspective of providing network quality intermediary, this paper analyzes and discusses the ideas and ways to solve the 'lemon' problem in the network market.

6.1 Introduction: Market Intermediary and Its Role

According to microeconomics, transaction intermediary is an indispensable element in market economy. Densetz [1] discussed the satisfaction conditions of intermediary for firms to achieve economies of scale and specialization from the perspective of transaction costs. He believed that intermediary is a necessary condition for firms to achieve economies of scale and specialization. According to traditional economics, the economic benefits provided by intermediaries depend to a great extent on the efficiency of the market organization. Whether intermediary can improve the efficiency of market operation depends on whether the total transaction cost and market transaction cost or coordination cost of using intermediary are higher than that of not using intermediary [3]. In order to make the company or market operate more efficiently, the product cost and transaction cost must be minimized. Therefore, the

Y. Pan, *Trust Management in the Chinese E-Commerce Market*,
Advanced Studies in E-Commerce, https://doi.org/10.1007/978-981-97-1115-4_6

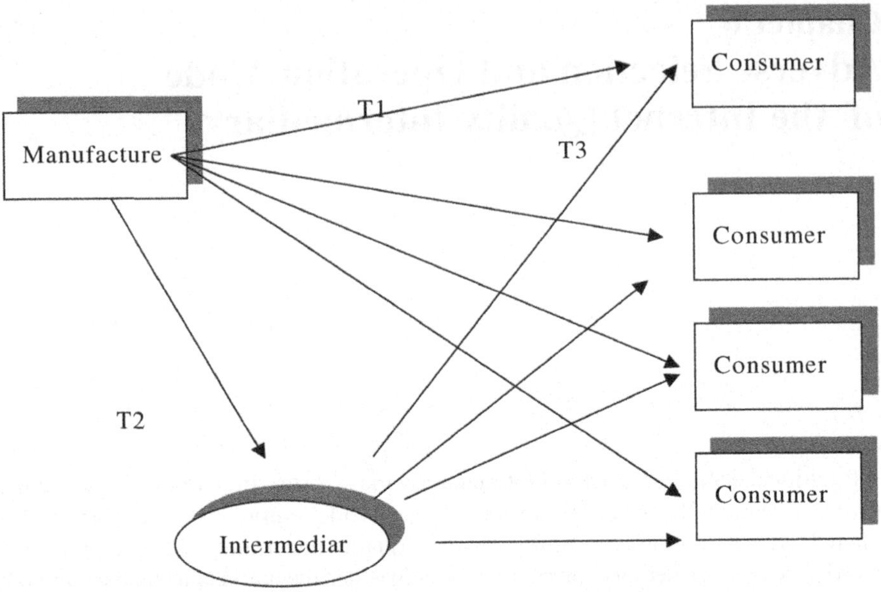

Fig. 6.1 Comparison of transaction costs with and without mediation[1]

market with low transaction cost operates more efficiently. Some people think that intermediaries increase distribution costs, but in fact, in order to deliver goods to customers in the physical market, using intermediaries can reduce inventory and transportation costs. It can be said that wholesalers and retailers provide producers with a more effective sales channel. Without these intermediaries, many companies will have to send products to every customer.

Choi et al. [2] illustrate the role of intermediation in both market environments through a graph (see Fig. 6.1). In the figure, if the manufacturer delivers the product directly to the consumer, each product needs to cost T_1. If the company wholesales the product to the intermediary, it needs to pay the intermediary fee T_2, but because the intermediary is close to the customer and has an efficient distribution system, the intermediary adds T_3 to its cost of sales as the final bid price. Therefore, the total transaction cost per product with intermediary participation is T_2 plus T_3, but it may still be lower than T_1, because the intermediary is closer to the customer, which reduces T_3. When manufacturers sell products by volume, only T_2 is added to the product cost, and the cost per product is actually reduced according to the economies of scale.

However, if products are retailed and distributed through intermediaries in the online market, their profits are not as obvious as those in the physical market. Because if an online company only sells a product to an intermediary, and the intermediary copies the product and then copies it to sell it to consumers, it is of little significance

[1] Reference to this figure: Choi, S.Y. et al. [1].

in digital commerce. The reason for this is that customers are very dispersed, and the cost T_3 of reselling products to consumers by intermediaries may be as large as the cost T_1 of direct transactions between manufacturers and customers. As a result, online sales intermediaries do not seem to play a role, especially in the process of product distribution. Therefore, the efficiency of e-commerce intermediary in market transactions is not very high. However, quality intermediary plays a particularly important role in e-commerce market, which is the problem we will discuss next.

6.2 Operation Model of Network Quality Mediation

6.2.1 *The Construction of Network Quality Intermediary Model*

We can use a model to explain the relationship between the quality intermediary in the network market and the network 'lemon' problem.

Suppose that there are multiple potential buyers and multiple potential buyers in the online market, and they are all risk neutral; The seller knows the quality of the products he sells θ; The 'lemon' principle tells us that because of the asymmetry of information, the buyer does not know the quality of each product, but can grasp the average quality of the product by means of speculation and experience. Therefore, we assume the quality distribution function $f(\theta)$ of the product.

Assuming that the buyer evaluates the value of the product as $v(\theta)$ and the seller evaluates the value of the product as $u(\theta)$. Obviously, there should be $\partial v/\partial\theta > 0$, and $\partial u/\partial\theta > 0$. If the buyer bids p and makes a deal, then the buyer's utility is $\pi_B = v(\theta) - p$ and the seller's utility is $\pi_S = p - u(\theta)$. Generally speaking, transactions occur because the buyer values the same item higher than the seller.

Therefore, we assume that $v(\theta) \geq u(\theta)$ (otherwise, the transaction is meaningless), and we define a difference coefficient $\varepsilon = v(\theta)/u(\theta)$, obviously $\varepsilon \geq 1$. For simplicity, let's assume that the buyer and the seller have the same preference and the seller's evaluation of the car is, that is, $(\theta) = \theta$, then there is: $v(\theta) = \varepsilon\theta$. Assuming that product quality θ is evenly distributed over $[a, b]$, i.e. the density function of product quality distribution is $(\theta) = \frac{1}{b-a}$, the relationship between average quality $\overline{\theta}$ and quality θ is:

$$\overline{\theta} = \frac{\theta + a}{2} \tag{6.1}$$

We use the demand curve to express the relationship between the price that buyers are willing to pay and the average quality of products in the market, and the supply curve to express the relationship between the average quality of products in the market and the price. In this way, we can get the demand curve and the supply curve with the average quality as independent variables.

The demand curve D is:

$$p(\overline{\theta}) = \varepsilon\overline{\theta} \tag{6.2}$$

The supply curve S is:

$$\overline{\theta} = \frac{\frac{1}{b-a}\int_a^p \theta d\theta}{\frac{1}{b-a}\int_a^p d\theta} = \frac{p+a}{2} =, \text{ or expressed as: } p = a - 2\overline{\theta} \tag{6.3}$$

Among them, $\overline{\theta} \in \left(a, \frac{a+b}{2}\right)$.

Combine (6.2) and (6.3), and the solution is $(\frac{a}{2-\varepsilon}, \frac{a\varepsilon}{2-\varepsilon})$, which is shown on the figure as the intersection of demand curve D and supply curve S, as shown in Fig. 6.2.

Because of $\overline{\theta}\in[a, \frac{a+b}{2}]$, the supply curve S in Fig. 6.2 is a line segment, and the corresponding abscissa region is a closed interval $[\overline{\theta}_1, \overline{\theta}_3]$. We can see from the figure that the intersection of the supply curve and the demand curve, that is, the equilibrium price and equilibrium quality of the transaction ε are increasing functions. In this way, we can achieve three situations:

[Case 1] Under normal circumstances, the intersection of supply curve S and demand curve D_2 (as shown in B in the figure) reflects the size of network transaction volume and transaction price, but under the condition of adverse selection, it will make all $\theta > \frac{a}{2-\varepsilon}$ products remain in the hands of sellers.

[Case 2] When the ε maximum value is reached, when S and D_3 intersect at point A $(\overline{\theta}_3, p_3)$, the transaction price and transaction quality are the highest, and the transaction volume is larger;

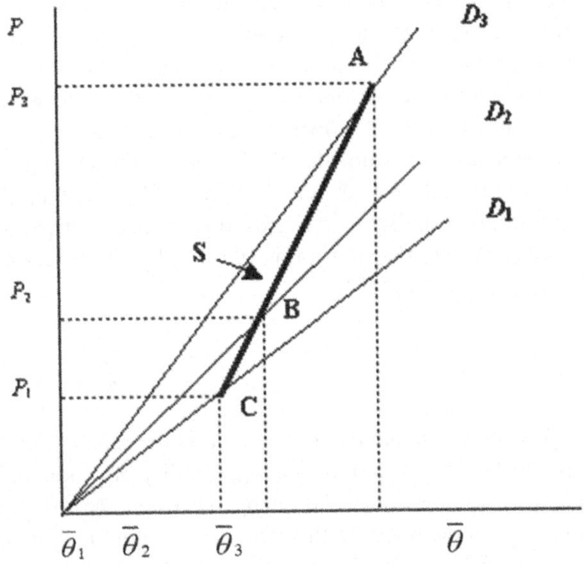

Fig. 6.2 Operation of network quality mediation

[Case 3] When $\varepsilon = 1$, the intersection of S and D_1 is C $(\overline{\theta}_0, p_0)$, the transaction price and transaction quality are the lowest, and the transaction volume is also the smallest.

Obviously, the transaction efficiency of these three cases depends on the size. Comparatively, although the first transaction has the influence of adverse selection, its transaction price and transaction quality are the highest and the transaction volume is larger, while the third transaction efficiency is the lowest, even inefficient. However, the particularity of online transactions is that they tend to be low-priced transactions, so the third situation will be more likely to happen. Therefore, the task of quality intermediary is to try to make point B approach point A (instead of point C), so as to improve the efficiency of market transactions.

Assuming that the network quality intermediary collects commissions m_1 and m_2 from buyers and sellers respectively, the currency price of both parties at the time of transaction is still P, and the cost of the intermediary itself is c, then the income of the intermediary is:

$$\pi_m = m_1 + m_2 - c$$

The utility of the buyer becomes:

$$\pi_B = v(\theta) - p - m_1$$

The seller's utility becomes:

$$\pi_S = p - u(\theta) - m_2$$

The net social welfare is:

$$\begin{aligned} \pi_n &= \pi_B + \pi_S + \pi_m \\ &= (v(\theta) - p - m_1) + (p - u(\theta) - m_2) + m_1 + m_2 - c \\ &= (\varepsilon - 1)\theta - c \end{aligned} \tag{6.4}$$

Obviously, the necessary conditions for the existence of network quality intermediary are:

$$\underset{B \to A}{Max\theta} \tag{6.5}$$

$$0 < (\varepsilon - 1)\theta - c \tag{6.6}$$

6.2.2 Conclusion

Through the analysis of the above models, we can draw the following conclusions:

[Conclusion 1] The improvement of network transaction efficiency depends on the relationship of three variables: the quality distribution of network products, the cost of network intermediary and the difference between buyers and sellers in the utility evaluation of the same item. Quality intermediary should be the link between the two sides of the transaction.

[Conclusion 2] From formula (6.4), it can be seen that the social net welfare level of the whole network market has nothing to do with the costs paid by buyers and sellers (m_1 and m_2) and the transaction price p. Therefore, as long as the intermediary cost c can increase the recognition coefficient to a certain extent ($\overline{\theta} > \frac{c}{2(\varepsilon-1)} + a$), the efficiency of market transactions can be improved, that is, the welfare level of the whole society can be improved. The increase of intermediary cost c should belong to the increase of transaction cost, but it also increases the efficiency of the market, otherwise, the transaction volume will decrease or even have no transaction volume.

One of the decisive reasons why online intermediaries can solve the 'lemon' problem by providing quality information is that intermediaries can sell products from many manufacturers. If the intermediary of a single product can collude with the manufacturer to share profits and continue to sell despite the complaints of consumers, when the intermediary of multiple products colludes with a supplier and continues to sell the problematic products, consumers will stop buying other products of this intermediary at the same time. They need to sell the quality information of products or services as products, and provide reliable information to customers to maintain their reputation. This mechanism of 'information spillover' will encourage manufacturers to maintain high quality by prompting intermediaries to stop selling products of unethical manufacturers and penalizing them. Therefore, as long as the new transaction costs can increase the welfare level of the whole society, effective intermediaries will still exist for a long time in the era of network economy.

[Conclusion 3] It is impossible to completely eliminate the influence of 'lemon' problem on market efficiency. What we have to do is to increase the degree and quantity of transactions as much as possible, that is, to reduce the negative influence of adverse selection on market transaction volume, that is, to reduce the products left in the hands of sellers with a quality distribution of $\theta > \frac{a}{2-\varepsilon}$.

[Conclusion 4] It can be seen from formula (6.5) and Fig. 6.2 that the more network products with larger quality distribution, the more quality intermediary is needed.

6.3 Adverse Selection and Network Quality Mediation

The development of e-commerce has changed the original business operation mode and greatly shortened the distance between the two parties in time and space, but adverse selection has greatly reduced the market transaction efficiency of e-commerce. In order to successfully complete the transaction and improve the transaction efficiency of the market, it is necessary for third-party institutions or organizations to intervene and provide authentic and reliable information for both parties, including product quality, price and credit of the parties. Because the means of solving information asymmetry in network market is different from that in traditional market, we should pay special attention to the role of network quality intermediary when some effective methods in traditional market fail.

In the 'virtual market' produced by the network business model, although there are many different phenomena from the physical market, the market participants are still no more than sellers, buyers and middlemen. The emergence of cybermediary or third-party intermediary lies in the asymmetry of information between buyers and sellers, which requires its services to create value. In fact, network middlemen, that is, quality information brokers, can play an important role in the network market, and it can play a particularly important role in reducing the uncertainty of network product quality. Quality information brokers evaluate the quality of some products in order to maximize profits. Although they participate in the market, they do not consume products themselves. Therefore, in the market where buyers and sellers cannot fully solve the quality uncertainty, the market mechanism based on network intermediary can be more effective than the market mechanism without intermediary or rule system. Network middlemen will not disappear, but will create more market opportunities.

In addition, we can also use legal means to ensure that these network quality intermediaries provide true quality information. For example, there should be certain punishment measures for commercial organizations with poor goodwill and fraudulent acts. For a commercial organization that has committed serious fraud, its business license shall be revoked.

At present, the important quality intermediaries are CA, Certificate Authority (CA) and expert intermediaries.

E-commerce demonstration, that is, 'certification body', is the body responsible for issuing certificates, authenticating certificates, managing issued certificates, formulating policies and concrete steps to verify and identify users' identities and signing users' certificates to ensure the identity of certificate holders and the ownership of public keys. Generally speaking, CA is a third-party online identity authentication institution that is trusted, recognized, authoritative and does not participate in transactions by various industries, departments and the public. It can be authorized by the government or other institutions. For example, websites such as Alibaba (http://www.alibaba.com) and Dun & Bradstreet (http://Dun & Bradstreet) provide online credit files for buyers and sellers engaged in e-commerce, and combine the characteristics of traditional authentication services and network interaction to help enterprises gain the trust of online transactions from the perspective of third-party authentication.

The expert intermediary plays a greater role in solving the 'lemon' problem in the network market. The development of China's e-commerce industry needs more quality intermediaries, and more trustworthy quality intermediaries. Successful electronic intermediary enterprises need to carefully design its system rules and strategies to ensure the correctness of product information. Below, AUCNET.COM, a used car online auction agency in Japan, takes a case to illustrate this problem.

Case: Quality Assurance System of AUCNET.COM Company in Japan.[2]

Japan's AUCNET Company is a world-famous used car online auction intermediary company. It was founded in 1985 by a used car dealer named Fujisaki, and mainly provides information on the used car market. AUCNET's system is a centralized online wholesale market, which mainly serves used car dealers all over Japan. Only those subscription dealers who pay a certain monthly fee will be allowed to enter AUCNET.

AUCNET has created the world's largest car auction market without parking spaces. Its main function is to play the role of a quality intermediary. Although advanced technical conditions are necessary for the success of AUCNET Company, the innovation of AUCNET Company in system and rules ensures the product quality in the transaction process and reduces the adverse selection faced by consumers.

Members of AUCNET participate in the auction mainly because they believe AUCNET's guarantee of product quality, or believe that the information it provides is more true. The company's main measures are: (1) product classification, evaluation and inspection. Although AUCNET provides detailed information about the cars being auctioned, the seller of used cars must ask AUCNET's own technicians to inspect the cars and then classify them. AUCNET divides the quality rating of cars into 10 grades (the highest score is 10, and the lowest score is 1). If a used car scores less than 4 points, AUCNET will refuse to auction. The company has strict testing methods and systems, for example, it developed AIS (Automobile Inspection System), and uses Auc-Eye to improve the accuracy of testing. (2) Constraint and punishment of electronic contract. Every dealer participating in AUCNET transaction must sign an electronic contract with it, which stipulates the specific contents such as participants' responsibilities and settlement payments, and also specifies the implementation process of the electronic contract in detail. For example, the contract stipulates that if the seller successfully sells the car through AUCNET, he must hand over the car to the buyer on the day of the transaction or the next day, otherwise, he will be fined heavily (and finally handed over to the buyer) or even expelled from the market. On the other hand, if the buyer cancels the electronic transaction or delays payment, he will also be fined. Because AUCNET has a high reputation in Japan, deducting the right to use members is a very severe punishment. (3) Cultivate

[2] The content of this case comes from the company website (http://www.aucnet.co.jp/), Ma Jun [4] and Choi et al. [2].

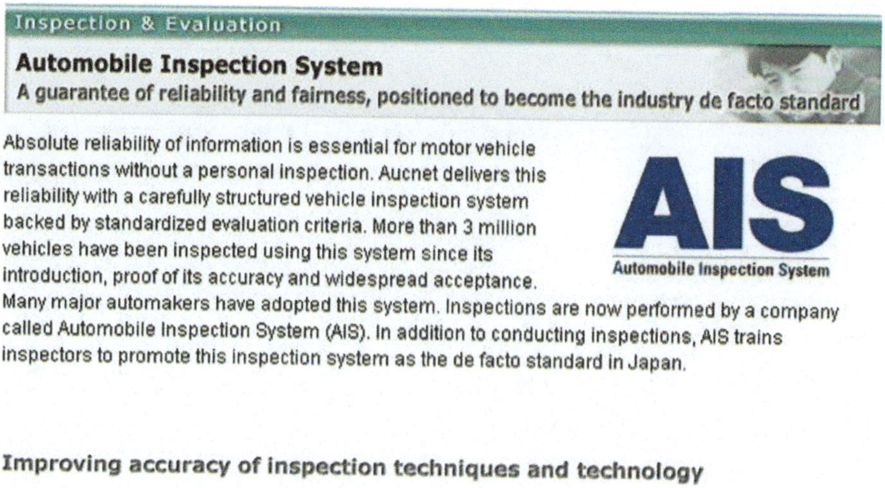

Fig. 6.3 AUCNET's Web page on testing and evaluation system

members' trust in AUCNET. For example, AUCNE also provides bulletin boards for its members to trade with. Just as market selection makes stock investors and commodity traders guarantee each other, this second-hand trading makes the market more active and helps traders build trust in the company (Fig. 6.3).

References

1. Densetz H (1968) The Cost of Transacting. The Quart J Econ: 33–35
2. Choi SY, Stahl DO, Whinston AB (1997) The economics of electronic commerce. Macmillan Technical Publishing, Indianapolis
3. Coase R (1937) The nature of the firm. Economica 4(1):386–405
4. Ma J, Wang S, Li J (2003) Theory and practice of online auction. Science Press, Beijing

Chapter 7
Adverse Selection and Non-economic Solutions

Eventually, according to Akerlof's [1] analysis, the used car market would disappear altogether, but this did not happen. As a matter of fact, in recent years, the trade of used cars has become increasingly popular in the world when the sales of new cars are generally booming. From the situation in developed countries, the annual transaction volume of used cars is only high or low compared with new cars. For example, in the United States, the transaction volume of used cars was roughly equal to that of new cars in 1993. In 1995, the sales volume of used cars exceeded that of new cars, and it has been on the rise in recent years. In 1998, 9 million people bought cars in Britain, of which 1.9 million bought new cars and 7 million bought old cars (Skouse and Taylor (2). Why is this happening? In fact, in addition to the methods and ways to solve adverse selection mentioned earlier, another important reason is that the system is perfect. For example, many States in the United States have passed legislation on 'used cars' (also known as 'Lemon Law'), and manufacturers' guarantees are more perfect and take longer. The existence of these laws and better guarantees creates an atmosphere of greater trust, even if these measures are not used by a particular buyer, as both buyers and sellers in the used car market know. Therefore, sellers bring better cars to the used car market, and more buyers participate. This fact shows that solving adverse selection requires not only economic means, but also non-economic means.

In fact, Professor Akerlof[1] himself has studied the interaction between social customs and markets in papers in 1980 and 1983. Among them, the second article focuses on the role of instilling moral principles, and uses theoretical examples to illustrate the principles that parents want to give to their children. Bond's [4] experimental study of Akerlof model also shows that the influence of used cars and new cars on the market lies not in the 'new' and 'old' cars, but in the role of offset system, as well as the efficiency and cost of search. Therefore, it is very necessary to explore the non-economic means to solve the network adverse selection.

---

[1] Akerlof [3].

Y. Pan, *Trust Management in the Chinese E-Commerce Market*,
Advanced Studies in E-Commerce, https://doi.org/10.1007/978-981-97-1115-4_7

7.1 Introduction: The Game Model of Product Quality and Its Enlightenment

In the model of 'lemon market', Akerlof proves that under the condition of adverse selection, there will be market failure and the Gresham phenomenon that 'inferior products drive out good products'.[2] However, if we regard the 'lemon' problem as a prisoner's dilemma in which buyers and sellers play games in the marketand play games indefinitely, the conclusion may change. Let's explain the relationship between adverse selection and system through a game process.

7.1.1 *The Game Model of Product Quality*

We refer Heal model[3] to analyze the product quality game in the e-commerce market. Consider two traders, x and y, who are endowed with the total inventory of two products, x or y, respectively. The quality of the same product is not exactly the same, and can be divided into high-quality products and low-quality products (correspondingly, y is also divided into high-quality products and low-quality products). Only the owner of inventory can distinguish between high-quality goods and low-quality goods. Let us assume that a unit x and a unit y are exchanged equivalently, and at the same time, suppose that all possible benefits of x to the transaction are: the utility of getting a unit of high-quality y is u_1, the utility of getting a unit of low-quality y is u_2, the utility of selling a unit of high-quality x is v_1, and the utility of selling a unit of low-quality x is v_2.

At the same time, suppose y is priced in the same way as X and y are exchanged, and the rest are priced exactly the same as X. Then each trader has two strategic choices, that is, selling high-quality products or selling low-quality products. Their payments are shown in Fig. 7.1:

If $u_1 + v_2 > v_1 + u_1$ and $u_2 + v_2 > u_2 + v_1$, that is, when $v_2 > v_1$, X will choose to trade with a low-quality product X, and this premise will also lead y to choose to provide X with a low-quality y. Of course, both v_2 and v_1 are negative here. Thus, we can conclude that low-quality products will drive out high-quality products as long as trading a unit of low-quality products will cause less loss of utility to traders than trading a unit of high-quality products. If we complicate the conditions of the

[2] 'Prisoner's Dilemma' is a classic example of game theory and economic game theory. It refers to a situation where both parties seek their own interests under non-cooperative conditions, which makes their situation worse. It was first named by Albert Tucker in an unpublished article. Suppose there are two prisoners, A and B, who were arrested for committing crimes together. The prosecutor talked with each prisoner separately, and the prosecutor said: If both confess, each will be sentenced to 8 years; if both deny it, each will be sentenced to one year; if one of them confesses and the other denies it, he will be released frankly, and he will be sentenced to 10 years if he does not confess. As a result, both of them chose to confess and were sentenced to eight years in prison because they positioned their strategy on the basis of confession and denial by others.

[3] Heal [5].

		Y's strategy	
		High quality	Low quality
X's strategy	High quality	v_1+u_1, v_1+u_1	u_2+v_1, u_1+v_2
	Low quality	u_1+v_2, u_2+v_1	u_2+v_2, u_2+v_2

Fig. 7.1 Product quality game of *X* and *Y*

example, for example, by differentiating pricing the possible different situations of the transactions of two traders *X* and *Y*, the conclusion is exactly equivalent to $v_2(X) > v_1(X)$ and $v_2(Y) > v_1(Y)$.

If the exchange of products is regarded as an uncooperative game, then a Nash Equilibrium of the game is a combination of strategies (low quality, low quality), which is the effect of the 'prisoner problem'. But now let us suppose that when traders want to trade not only once, but to trade with each other once at each stage and continuously in subsequent time periods, the game we face is a super game, that is, a game that is repeated indefinitely many times.

We can consider the following strategic combination: if *X* trades with quality goods in the first stage, and trades with inferior goods in the first stage ($t > 1$) if and only if *Y* trades with inferior goods in the previous stage (called strategy SX). For *Y*, you only need to replace *X* in SX with *Y*, and the rest will remain unchanged (strategy SY).

Let both parties discount future earnings at a discount rate of $\delta\,(0 < \delta < 1)$, and return to the original example. If *Y* implements strategy SY and *X* also implements strategy SX, then *X*'s income is:

$$(v_1 + u_1)\sum_{t=1}^{\infty}\delta^t \tag{7.1}$$

If *Y* implements strategy SY, *X* will break away from strategy SX, and implement 'high-quality products' strategy from $T = 1$ to $T = T$, but he adopts 'low-quality' strategy at $T + 1$ stage. Since *Y* adopts SY strategy, he will start to implement 'low-quality' strategy from $T + 2$ stage, so the best strategy *X* can adopt is to sell inferior products. Therefore, the highest benefit that *X* can get from breaking away from SX from $T + 1$ stage is:

$$(v_1 + u_1)\sum_{t=1}^{T}\delta^t + (u_1 + v_2)\delta^{T+1} + (u_2 + v_2)\sum_{t=T+2}^{\infty}\delta^t \tag{7.2}$$

We want to know whether it is better for *X* to continue SX or break away from SX. That is, we want to know whether the difference between (7.1) and (7.2) is positive or negative. According to derivation and calculation, if and only if the following conditions are met, the difference between the two formulas is positive, that is, there are:

$$\delta > \frac{v_2 - v_1}{u_1 - u_2} \tag{7.3}$$

7.1.2 The Conclusion

From the above game process, we can see that as long as the (7.3) formula is satisfied, the strategic combination (SX, SY) forms a Nash Equilibrium, and we can expect that only high-quality products can participate in the transaction in the market. With the increase of δ, the weight given to future earnings also increases, so as the weight given to future earnings by traders increases, the chances of inferior products driving out high products are decreasing. In other words, only when traders are short-sighted enough can we say with certainty that inferior products drive out high-quality products, otherwise, market participants are willing to trade with high-quality products. Among them, the δ value depends on a proportional value, that is, the utility difference between selling inferior products and selling superior products and the utility difference between obtaining superior products and obtaining inferior products.

So, is the above game process contradictory to Akerlof model? Is Professor Akerlof's conclusion wrong? In fact, this conclusion does not contradict the 'lemon market' model. Because the occurrence of this game must be guaranteed by corresponding mechanisms—this mechanism is different from economic means, which may be laws, regulations or moral norms—it is a non-economic means. Only with the guarantee of non-economic means can the market participants have a cooperative game in order to avoid the market failure caused by the 'lemon' problem.[4]

Recently, some economists are still discussing the role of non-economic means. For example, Hendel and Lizzei [6, 7] emphasized the role of non-market institutions in solving asymmetric information problems in the process of dynamic analysis of 'lemon market' model. The above conclusions are very enlightening for us to study the adverse selection of online market.

7.2 Adverse Selection and Government Means

Adverse selection theory proves to us that under the condition of imperfect information, market mechanism cannot operate effectively and resources cannot be allocated optimally. Liberal and conservative economists differ widely on whether and how much government should play in addressing information imperfections. However,

[4] It should be pointed out that although game theory provides us with a powerful analytical tool for studying reputation management. However, many reputation models in game theory pay more attention to the information asymmetry of players, while ignoring the cost factors of the game process and the institutional conditions needed to ensure the game to go on.

whether economists agree or not, governments play different roles in solving information imperfections to varying degrees in practice. In addition to using 'Lemon Law', Trademark Law and Property Law to provide consumers with as perfect information as possible, the government also requires companies to provide consumers with a series of information, including company management information, financial reports, product side effects and so on. These effective government means can be used for reference in our analysis and discussion to solve the problem of network adverse selection.

7.2.1 The 'Lemon Law' and the Relevant Laws of E-Commerce

Let's take a look at the 'lemon method' first. In view of the 'lemon' flood in the used car market, which seriously harms the interests of consumers, many American States try to use legal means to protect consumers. Among them, the most famous[5] is the 'Lemon Law' passed by California. The Lemon Act of New York State has been in force since 1983. By 1990, 12 carmakers had refunded up to $1 billion to New York City car owners [8].

As a non-economic means, 'Lemon Law' plays a very important role in protecting the interests of consumers and improving the efficiency of market transactions. Of course, 'Lemon Law' also encountered many practical problems in the process of implementation, such as high legal fees and different state laws when old cars crossed different states. The example of 'Lemon Law' shows that legal means can be used as a supplement to economic means to reduce the information asymmetry faced by consumers. This idea can be extended to the network market. In this respect, the situation in the United States can provide us with some enlightenment.

The United States is one of the origins of the global Internet. Since the mid-1990s, in order to promote and guarantee the all-round development of e-commerce, most states in the United States have formulated e-commerce laws. For example, Utah Digital Signature Act promulgated in 1995. In addition to the main e-commerce laws, some States also have some supporting laws and regulations. For example, Illinois has the Financial Institutions Digital Signature Act in addition to the Illionis Electronic Commerce Security Act; Florida has a Digital Signature & Electronic Notarization Act in addition to the Electronic Signature Act. From the name of legal

[5] The 'Lemon Law' stipulates that this law can be applied to used cars purchased from dealers for more than $1,500, with a mileage of 100,000 miles, which were originally non-commercial vehicles and have been out of the factory for two years or traveled more than 18,000 miles. The warranty period varies from 30 to 90 days according to mileage. During any warranty project, you can ask the dealer to repair it free of charge, even change cars and refund money. The Act states that if a used car has been repaired four times a year for the same problem after sale, or has been placed in a garage for at least 30 days, the used car dealer must buy the car back, repair it after re-sale, and label it 'lemon buy-back' to inform the new buyer (http://www.pcaauto.com.cn/price/csrm/10207/706.html).

documents, some are called Electronic Commerce Act, such as North Carolina and South Carolina; some are called the Electronic Commerce Security Act, such as Iowa and Illinois; another is called Electronic Author-Cation Act. Among them, 'Electronic Signature Act' and 'Digital Signature Act' are the most legal names. In addition, the United States Uniform Computer Information Transactions Act (UCITA) also defines the examination of standard clauses and the rights and obligations of both parties in e-commerce, with the purpose of drawing consumers' attention to the standard clauses and ensuring the fairness of electronic transactions.[6] The bill is supported by most software manufacturers and publishers. Although there is no specific online 'lemon law' in the current e-commerce legislation, these laws are the first step to alleviate consumers' concerns and reduce online fraud.

China's laws and regulations such as Consumer Protection Law, Product Quality Law and Contract Law have established the consumer protection system under the condition of traditional consumption contract. However, in the case of e-commerce, due to its differences from traditional transactions and traditional consumption contracts, it may have characteristics different from traditional markets. China's first systematic e-commerce regulation 'Guangdong Province Electronic Transaction Regulations', which came into effect in February 2003,[7] has made a good start in this respect. The regulations set up a special chapter to stipulate 'certification institutions' and clarify their rights and obligations. At present, Shanghai, Guangdong, Beijing and other places have launched e-commerce certification to varying degrees.

7.2.2 Administrative Means

Besides law, administrative means can also play a very important role in eliminating and reducing adverse selection. The United States Department of Commerce [9] and the United Nations Organization for Economic Cooperation and Development (OECD) [10, 11] have expressed strong concern for the security and confidentiality of e-commerce transactions. In the United States, consumers can report suspected fraud to the judicial authorities and ask for judicial relief. At the same time, American government agencies have begun to formulate corresponding administrative measures to regulate the behavior of online manufacturers and give advice to

[6] Article 39 of China's Contract Law defines standard clauses: 'Standard clauses are clauses drawn up in advance by the parties for repeated use and not negotiated with the other party when concluding a contract'. The contract in e-commerce is characterized in that the operator formulates all the clauses, and the consumer only needs to press the 'accept' or 'reject' key to decide whether the purchase contract is established or not. Some operators set the following terms on their websites: 'Press the accept button to indicate that you have agreed to the following conditions.' Generally speaking, if consumers want to register successfully, they can only press the 'Accept' button. Usually, consumers usually only have the opportunity to read these terms at the time of registration, and these terms do not appear in the transaction process in subsequent transactions. Many websites also declare the right to modify the terms of service at any time, which puts consumers in a passive position (http://www.econsumer.gov/english/).

[7] http://www.jcrb.com.cn/zyw/n1/ca17329.htm.

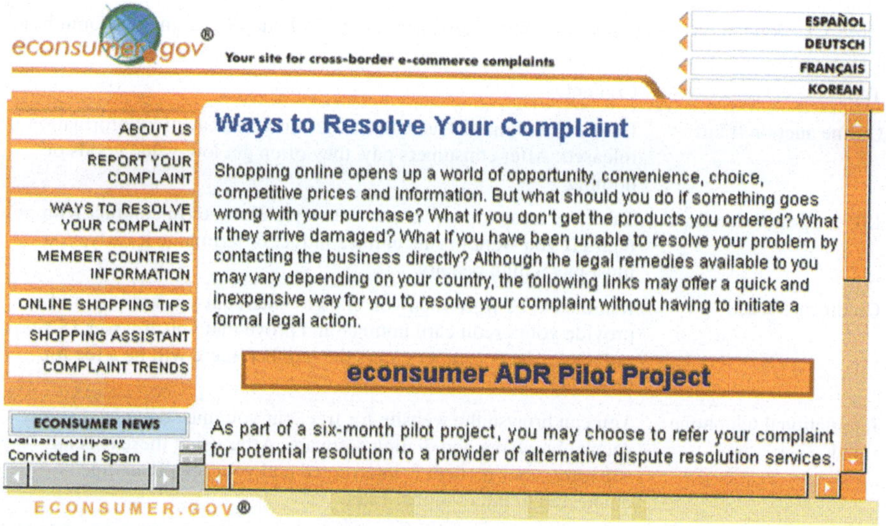

Fig. 7.2 Related pages of the Federal Trade Commission (FTC) website

consumers. For example, The Federal Trade Commission[8] (FTC) specifically accepts complaints from online consumers and alerts them (see Fig. 7.2).

Based on consumer complaints, FTC has made relevant analysis using the Committee's complaint database, and summarized the top ten online commercial frauds (see Table 7.1).

The council also advises all online consumers: (1) Don't trust merchants' propaganda and promises of potential profits easily, and study the contract carefully before signing the contract. (2) Pay attention to all the words and links of merchants, because fraudsters often use the carelessness of visitors to consciously hide 'secrets' in the words and links. (3) Pay attention to the privacy clause. If the merchant does not provide or is vague, he must give up the transaction. (4) Enterprises that fail to provide their detailed residence, business address and telephone number on the website must be highly vigilant.

7.2.3 *Morality and Moral Norms*

Morality and moral norms are also non-economic means to solve the 'lemon' problem. Morality has been studied for more than 2,500 years, and the focus of discussion is the analysis and description of its basic concepts, who is right and who is wrong on this issue, and how to judge around these different viewpoints. These topics must include the examination of responsibilities, rights and obligations. A particularly important aspect of moral requirements is the study of professional activities.

[8] http://www.ftc.gov/.

Table 7.1 Top ten online commercial frauds summarized by the Federal Commerce Commission (FTC)

Type	Content
Online auction fraud	Using virtual market as bait, a large amount of auction information is released. After consumers pay, they often get low-value goods or nothing
ISP access service fraud	Take free as an attractive means to sign a long-term contract with them. If you want to cancel the contract or terminate it early, you must pay a high penalty
Credit card fraud	It claims to be free when you click to enter, but you are required to provide your credit card number and prove that you are over 18 years old. Once the consumer enters the number, there will be a fee for browsing
International telephone fraud	You can browse the website for free, but you must download some special browsing and dialing software. After using these special software, your modem is interrupted and your telephone line is connected to international calls
Free website fraud	Free use of personal websites for a period of time without having to bear the obligation to pay. But even if consumers don't use it overtime, they will be billed by telephone
Network pyramid selling fraud	Like pyramid selling, we make money by developing offline. But at this time, the offline is the network carefully planned by the merchants themselves or merchants. Once consumers enter the network, they are trapped
Online travel fraud	With low-cost travel or 'zero tour fare' as bait, travel agencies put forward various hidden fees and increased fees after travelers go to the tour
Network entrepreneurship fraud	Put forward a grand business plan to ensure that you can get high returns. But it was a complete hoax
Network investment fraud	Merchants ask you to participate in venture capital and promise to get a quick return. But they are often deceived
Selling fake drugs online	Claiming that their drugs are not yet on the market, but can cure serious or terminal diseases. But in fact, the drug has no effect on serious illness at all

Traditionally, some norms and reasonable and fair systems are mostly constructed by a group of individuals with professional skills or knowledge. Moral standards not only adjust people's inner activities, but also influence people's external behaviors. To a great extent, they show their consistency and credibility to the society, which is conducive to maintaining the stability and unity of a certain industry. In this way, morality is not only a tool of pragmatic views, but also a necessary factor of professional consistency.

The rapid development of network economy poses a fundamental challenge to all professional norms including marketing ethics. The characteristics of the revolution in computer technology reflect the extent of this demand. Compared with other major technological advances such as printing and publishing, telephone, automobile and digital media, the speed, universality and diversity of computer technology are unique. These factors lead to a vacuum in ethics. Although these rapid developments do not directly challenge the general principles of fairness and honesty, the progress of digital technology and its potential development make moral and other norms have to change themselves to adapt to the new changes of the computer revolution.

The American Marketing Association (AMA) has issued relevant content to promote ethics and beliefs in response to fraud in the online market. These requirements include: Working members are prohibited from dealing with clients or third parties in doubt, especially those with financial credibility, and their licensees are required to strictly abide by legal and ethical agreements and revoke cases of harm. The content issued by AMA has played a role in inspiring consumers' trust. Another method of dealing specifically with ethical aspects of online transactions is educational encouragement for all consumers. Professional associations have the ability to create such websites, propose and explain the minimum standards of consumer protection, and increase the cleanliness of online transactions through their reporting and exposure of behaviors that undermine laws and ethics.

The rapid development of network, the construction of morality and law, and the mutual influence between them are equivalent to the changes among technology, economy and society. As a participant in the space of the network, it is not only necessary to formulate these rules well, but also to accept these norms of behavior gladly, so as to contribute to the globalization in the electronic age.

7.3 Adverse Selection and Internet Trust

Solving the problem of adverse selection is actually the process of eliminating information uncertainty, and the analysis in the previous chapters also explores solutions around this core. It should be pointed out that trust, as the recognition and acceptance of a social order, plays an irreplaceable role as an economic means in solving the Internet 'lemon' problem, and has important significance. It can be said that establishing and advocating Internet trust is the ethical basis for solving Internet adverse selection.

7.3.1 The Definition and Essence of Trust

Many scholars have given different definitions and understandings about the definition of trust. Duetsh [12] believes that trust is the expectation of events. Schlenker (13) believes that trust is the result of believing the description of uncertain information environment received from others and accepting and believing this information under risky circumstances. According to Remple and Holmes (14), trust is the probability of expecting events to happen in the future. Brock (15) defines customer trust as maintaining the belief and expectation that the entrusted person can fulfill the entrusted person, and showing the willingness to present his weaknesses to others. Anderson and Narus [16] argue that trust can reduce the risk of buying and selling in a business relationship. Therefore, the trust tendency of users is the key factor for the success of buying and selling. Some scholars believe that trust is an important part of a healthy personality [17].

Zarker (18) divides trust into three types. One is process-based trust, which holds that the formation of trust is generated by the accumulation of past experience or continuous transactions; the second is trait-based trust, which holds that the formation of trust is caused by the similarity of characteristics, which may be caused by family background, race, gender and other factors; the third is institutional-based, that is, the formation of trust is produced by the formal social structure. Shapiro (19) divides trust according to authority, knowledge and sense of identity. He believes that authority-based trust comes from authority pressure; knowledge-based trust is obtained by knowledge collection, which allows understanding and predicting the behavior of the trusted person; identity-based trust is derived from the values shared by partners.

Sako (20) also divides trust into three types from the perspective of economics: first, Contractual trust, that is, the rules made by buyers and sellers, both parties must abide by their promises, and verbal promises are also a kind of contracts; the second is Competence trust from ability. In the relationship between buyers and sellers, trust comes from the seller's ability, including technical ability and management ability; the third is Goodwill trust. There is no clear commitment between the buyer and the seller, and the buyer's requirements are expected to be met.

Combining the above definitions and looking at trust from the perspective of economy and management, we can think that trust is the most basic element to maintain economic operation. No matter what the source of trust is, trust is actually the loyalty of consumers to enterprises or brands. Loyalty is the degree to which a customer has a positive attitude toward a brand, is committed to it and intends to continue buying in the future. Griffin (21) once pointed out that customers are the most important resources for enterprises. Loyal customers will not only bring income to enterprises, but also help enterprises spread a good corporate image. Loyal customers are not only single customers, but constantly make repeated purchases from the same company, build up the reputation of products, and have immunity to competitors' promotional activities. From the perspective of relationship marketing, trust is the central element of successful relationship marketing [22].

Table 7.2 Development mechanism of business trust process[9]

Stage of development	Action	Influencing factors
Calculation process	Calculate the cost or reward of cheating or maintaining a relationship with a trading partner, and guess whether the other party has the intention of cheating	Supplier's reputation, supplier's information sharing, supplier's transaction times, supplier's willingness to customize, buyer's past experience
Forecasting process	In this process, the repeated interactions between trading partners can provide a predictable basis to explain the behavior results of trading partners	The number and duration of transactions with the supplier, whether the buyer feels that the supplier is popular, and the buyer's past experience
Capability process	This process is mainly to judge whether trading partners are capable of implementing their commitments	Professional ability of suppliers
Intentional process	Trusters will try to explain the motives behind the actions of trustees. If both parties can develop shared values or norms, intentions will arise, and one trading partner will be prompted to understand the purpose of the other	Supplier information sharing, buyer's past experience
Transfer process	This process represents the transfer of trust from a trusted source of proof to another person or group with little or no direct experience with the principal	The reputation of the supplier, the buyer's trust in the supplier

7.3.2 *Trust Mechanism of Internet Transaction*

7.3.2.1 The Trust Mechanism in Traditional Ttransactions

The analysis and description of Doney and Cannon [23] reflect the evolving mechanism of the trust process (see Table 7.2).

Chow (24) explores the loyalty relationship between buyers and sellers by using trust factors, and establishes a trust model in the relationship between buyers and sellers (as shown in Fig. 7.3).

[9] Source: Doney and Cannon [23].

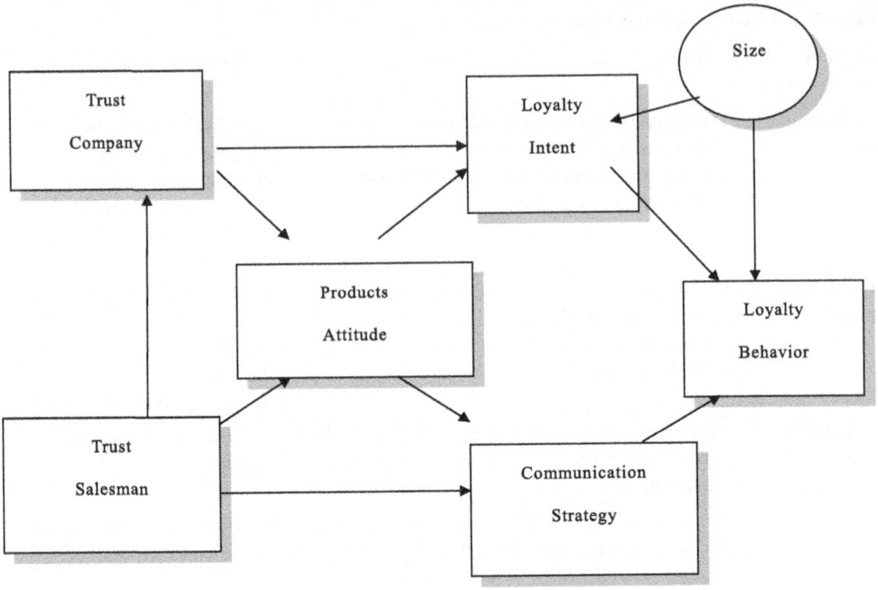

Fig. 7.3 Trust patterns in transactions[10]

7.3.2.2 The Trust Mechanism in Online Transactions

Kini and Choobineh [26] studied the sources of trust in e-commerce environment. They believe that the sources of trust in e-commerce environment are information environment, system, personal characteristics and work. Among them, the environment includes the display platform, organization and benefits, the system includes the security and dependability of the system; personal traits include whether trust tendency in personality is beneficial; operation refers to the risk of transaction. Based on this, a trust integration model in e-commerce environment is proposed (see Fig. 7.4).

Kini and Choobineh [26] model provides a theoretical basis for the factors affecting trust in e-commerce market. It includes four levels: personality traits, information systems in the Internet environment, tasks that must be performed in the transaction process and information environment. This model shows that in the Internet market, trust depends not only on the personality traits determined by the social moral environment and the mainstream value system, it also depends on the technical environment.

[10] Source: Chow and Reed [25].

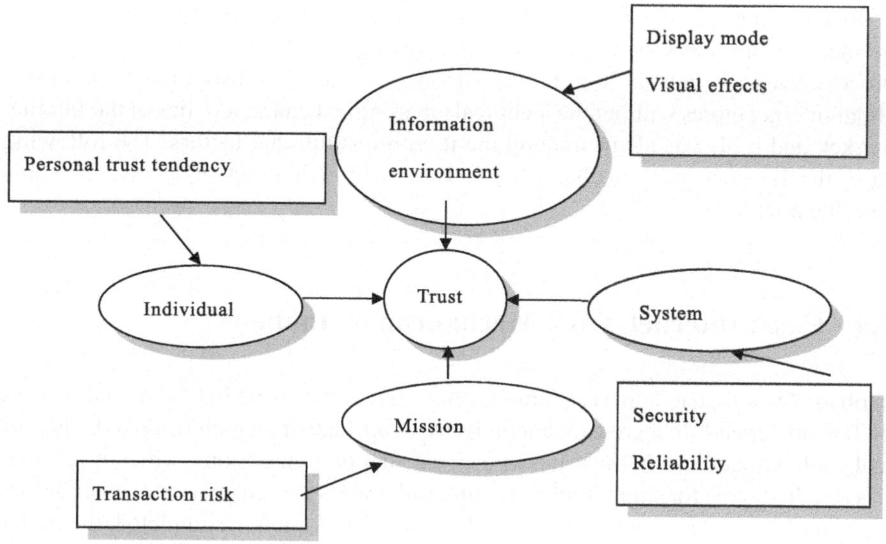

Fig. 7.4 Trust pattern in e-commerce environment[11]

7.3.2.3 Conclusion

To some extent, trust is a non-economic factor to solve the problem of adverse selection. It shows the recognition and acceptance of a social order or values, and it affects people's decision-making and judgment by affecting people's personality traits and other factors. With the development of the times and society, the form and content of trust will change. In addition to technical problems, the development of e-commerce also has problems in system and social psychology, which is the reconstruction of trust mechanism.

In October 2001, my8848, a well-known e-commerce website in China, was complained by many consumers because it was reflected that it received payment for goods ordered by consumers but did not deliver goods, and the quality was inconsistent with the price. Beijing Industrial and Commercial Bureau had to issue an urgent warning to consumers: Don't send money to my8848 for shopping, and advise people to choose cash on delivery for transactions. Although there[12] are many complicated reasons for this incident, such as self-operated mode, imperfect logistics system and the pursuit of click-through rate, it does reduce the trust of Chinese consumers in online transactions. Therefore, we must pay attention to trust as the core of the ethical culture environment to build, must understand the development of Internet trust and elements, otherwise, the solution of Internet adverse selection is not discussed.

---

[11] Source: Kini and Choobineh [26].

[12] Quoted from: Lun and Jianguo [27].

Establishing the trust mechanism of e-commerce is a very important and urgent problem in the development of Internet economy at present, and it also needs a process, even a relatively long process. However, it is obviously unrealistic to talk about Internet ethics without the technical environment characteristics of the Internet market, and it also needs us to combine it with institutional factors. The following case, the Internet trust mechanism of eBay auction Internet, may give us some enlightenment.

7.4 Case: Internet Trust Mechanism of Taobao[13]

Taobao (www.taobao.com) is a famous online auction website in China. The success of Taobao depends to a great extent on its trust mechanism, which records the historical credit situation of both parties in the past auction transactions, which is referred to as credit degree for short. Taobao requires all traders to register as a member before using the site for auction transactions. After the registration is completed, the trader becomes a registered user with an initial credit rating of zero.

The credit evaluation of Taobao is a system that users evaluate the interaction of trading objects according to the successful transaction on eBay Internet. Evaluation consists of evaluation types and comments. All the evaluations obtained by users constitute the credit records of users, which can provide reference for other users. If you are a buyer, Taobao requires you to carefully check the seller's credit history before bidding. You can judge whether the seller is honest and trustworthy, whether his goods are genuine and so on by other buyers' evaluation of the seller. If you are a seller, a good credit record will help you gain the trust of more buyers. When logging in items, you can select the buyer with higher credit rating in advance, and know what kind of transaction object the buyer is through the credit record of the buyer.

The auction process on Taobao is as follows: During the auction, you can browse the auctioneer's detailed description of the item and the bidding price, and you can also know the credit history of the auctioneer and all bidders in detail. Taobao not only provides each registered user's credit record for one month, six months and total, but also provides each registered user's credit evaluation after each auction transaction is completed, such as 'OK! Remittance is timely and transaction is quick!' Wait. After the auction transaction is completed, taobao will ask both parties to leave credit ratings for each other. No matter the winner or the auctioneer, their credit evaluation results can be attributed to good, medium or poor. After the credit evaluation is given, the new credit degree of the trader is equal to the original credit degree value plus the credit evaluation value obtained from this transaction. Finally, the trader's final credit rating is equal to the number of positive returns minus the number of negative returns per transaction. According to the credit quantity of each registered user, Taobao divides it into three grades: heart, diamond and crown grade, and the corresponding credit quantity ranges from 1 to 90, 91 to 2000, 2001 and above

[13] The case comes from the company's website http://www.taobao.com/.

Historical purchase behavior can accumulate the credit value of buyers and sellers, and the calculation method of credit value increase or decrease:

Authentication points: completed registration +1, real-name authentication +1, transaction information +1, totaling 3 points;

Bonus items: Taobao, Tmall shopping, each transaction +1;

Deduction items: Taobao and Tmall can deduct the credit points of buyers and sellers according to the violations and the number of violations of buyers

The reputation level is divided into three grades: heart, drill and crown, with five grades in each grade, totaling 15 reputation levels:

心钻冠	等级	分数
心	1心	1 ~ 3
	2心	4 ~ 10
	3心	11 ~ 20
	4心	21 ~ 50
	5心	51 ~ 90
钻	1钻	91 ~ 150
	2钻	151 ~ 250
	3钻	251 ~ 500
	4钻	501 ~ 1000
	5钻	1001 ~ 2000
冠	1冠	2001 ~ 5000
	2冠	5001 ~ 10000
	3冠	10001 ~ 20000
	4冠	20001 ~ 50000
	5冠	50001 ~

Fig. 7.5 The credit standard of taobao

respectively. If a registered user's credit rating reaches or is less than 0, its user name will be canceled. The credit rating and credit rating of all registered users on the Internet are made public (see Fig. 7.5).

The success of Taobao in China is largely due to its good credit system. To a certain extent, this mechanism reduces the problem of information asymmetry between the auction parties, so that buyers and sellers, as well as between them and auction websites, establish a mutual trust, and reduce the adverse selection faced by consumers. However, from the implementation situation, there are still some problems. For example, in order to get higher credit and credit rating as soon as possible, some auctioneers trade some low-value commodities in good faith at the initial stage of entering the auction market. When the credit degree and credit rating reach a higher level, some high-value commodities are auctioned in dishonesty by using the information asymmetry in auction market transactions, so as to obtain higher unfair gains. Auctioneers have the possibility of adverse selection because the total credit degree and credit rating do not reflect the actual value of the traded goods or the auction transaction price. It needs to continue to be studied and improved.

References

1. Akerlof GA (1970) The market for'lemon': qualitative uncertainty and the market mechanism. Quart J Econ 84(3):488–500
2. Mark Skousen Kenna C (1988) Taylor, Puzzles & Paradoxes in Economics. Edward Elgar Publishing
3. Akerlof GA (1980) A theory of social custom, of which unemployment may one consequence. Quart J Econ 94:749–775
4. Bond EW (1982) A direct test of the 'lemons 'model: the market for used pickup trucks. Am Econ Rev 72:836–840
5. Heal G (1976) Do bad products drive out good? Quart J Econ 90:499–502
6. Hendel I, Lizzeri A (1999) Adverse selection in durable goods. Markets American Economic Review 89(5):1097–1115
7. Hendel I, Lizzeri A (2002) The role of leasing under adverse selection. J Polit Econ 110:113–143
8. Song X (2002) Application of information economics in China after China's entry into WTO. Economic Trends 3:14–20
9. US Department of Commerce (1999) The emerging internet economy II. Secretariat on Electronic Commerce, US Department of Commerce, Washington, DC. http://www.ecommerce.gov
10. OECD (1997) Business-to-consumer electronic commerce:survey of status and issues. Head of Publication Services, Paris. OECD/GD(97)219. http://www.oecd.org/dsti/sti/it/ec
11. OECD (1997) The economic and social impact of electronic commerce: prelimimary findings and rearch agenda. Head of Publication Services, OECD, Paris. OECD code 931999001lP1. http://www.oecd.org/dsti/sti/it/ec
12. Duetsh M (1958) Trust and suspicion. J Conflict Resolut 2(4):265–279
13. Schlenker BR, Helm B, Tedeschi JT (1973) The Effects of Personality and Situational Variables on Behavioral Trust. J Personality and Social Psychology 25(3):419–427
14. Remple JK, Holmes JG, Zanna MP (1985) Trust in close relationships. Journal of Personality and Social Psychology 49:95–112
15. Brock WA, Hommes CH (1997) A Rational Route to Randomness. Econometrica 65(5):1059–95
16. Anderson JC, Narus JA (1990) A model of distributor firm and manufacturer firm working partnerships. J Mark 54:42–58
17. Lewicki JR, Mcallister JD, Bies RJ (1998) Trust and distrust: new relationships and realities. Acad Manag Rev 23(3):438–458
18. Zarker LG (1986) Production of Trust: Institutional Source of Electronic Structure,1984–1920. Research in Organizational Behavior, 8:55–111
19. Shapiro DL, Sheppard BH, Cherakin L (1992) Business On a Handshake. Negotiation Journal 8(4):365–377
20. Sako M (1992) Prices, quality, and trust:inter-firm relations in Britain and Japan. Cambridge University Press
21. Griffin J (1995) Customer Loyalty. How to Earn it and How to Keep it. Lexingtong Books, New York
22. Morgan RM, Hunt SD (1994) The commitment-trust theory of relationship marketing. J Mark 58:20–38
23. Doney PM, Cannon JP (1997) An examination of the nature of trust in buyer-seller relationships. J Mark 61(April):35–51
24. Chow S, Reed H (1997) Toward An Understanding of Loyalty: The Moderating Role of Trust. Journal of Management Issues 9(3):275–298
25. Chow S, Reed H (1997) Toward an understanding of loyalty: the modern role of trust. J Manag Issues 9(3):275–298

26. Kini A, Choobineh J (1998) Trust in electronic commerce: definition and theoretical considerations. IEEE
27. Lun L, Jianguo G (2002) Network trust crisis and ethical and cultural environment of e-commerce. J Soc Sci Xiangtan Univ 4:7–9

Chapter 8
Adverse Selection and Strategic Suggestions of Chinese E-Commerce Market

The main purpose of this chapter is to analyze the special performance of adverse selection in China's online transactions and the impact of adverse selection on Chinese netizens' consumer behavior. Because the content of this chapter is discussed after we analyze the general principles of adverse selection, we will take the characteristics of consumer behavior of Chinese netizens as the breakthrough point of analysis. As a special group, Internet users have different characteristics from traditional market groups. Therefore, in order to analyze the performance of adverse selection in China's online market, it is necessary to deeply understand the demand characteristics, purchase motivation and purchase behavior patterns of online users.

8.1 Consumer Behavior and Information Asymmetry

With the development of consumer society, the business concept of enterprises pays more and more attention to the changes of consumers. Since the 1960s, the management concept of enterprises has developed from production orientation and sales orientation to marketing orientation. Driven by the concept of marketing, the research on consumer behavior in the west has gradually developed.

Y. Pan, *Trust Management in the Chinese E-Commerce Market*,
Advanced Studies in E-Commerce, https://doi.org/10.1007/978-981-97-1115-4_8

8.1.1 Consumer Behavior and 'Stimulus–Response' Model

Generally speaking, consumer behavior can be regarded as composed of two parts: first, consumer action; the second is the purchasing decision-making process of consumers.[1] Purchasing decision is the psychological activity and behavior tendency of consumers before using and disposing of purchased products and services, which belongs to the formation process of consumption attitude. Consumer action is more a practical process of purchasing decision. In the real consumer life, these two parts of consumer behavior permeate and influence each other, and together constitute a complete process of consumer behavior.

Kolter (1) pointed out that the consumer buying behavior begins with the 'stimulus–response' model. The so-called consumer purchase behavior refers to the final purchase behavior of consumers. If you draw a stage model with a purchase process, it includes five stages: need recognition, information research, evolution of alternatives, purchase decision and post-purchase behavior. Among them, the main contents of each stage are as follows: (1) Demand confirmation: when consumers feel that there is a difference between their ideal state and their actual situation, they will have demand cognition; the factors that induce demand cognition may be personal internal needs or external stimuli. (2) Information collection: Once consumers confirm the existence of problems, they will collect more information. Its information sources can be divided into four types, including personal sources, commercial sources, public sources and experience sources. (3) Scheme evaluation: It includes: (i) Evaluative Criteria:

It is usually expressed by certain attributes or specifications, and the evaluation criteria are formed by personal accumulated information and experience on the one hand, and influenced by personal motivation on the other hand. (ii) Belief: Consumers' evaluation of various schemes or brands on various evaluation criteria. (iii) Attitude: The evaluation of consumers' comprehensive schemes or brands on various evaluation criteria will produce favorable or unfavorable reactions to the consistency of various schemes or brands. (iv) Intention: the subjective probability of consumers choosing a specific scheme or brand. (4) Purchase decision: The intention or preference formed by consumers in the evaluation stage will be implemented at this stage. (5) Post-purchase behavior: When you buy a product, there will be two situations (satisfaction or post-purchase disorder). When consumers find that their choices are consistent or satisfied with their beliefs, this experience will be loaded into their memory, which will affect future purchase decisions and increase the probability of repurchasing; if you feel dissatisfied, you will be out of balance and affect your future decision-making.

---

[1] As far as the research level is concerned, Western scholars usually divide the research on consumer behavior into macro and micro levels. Macro-level mainly studies the relationship between consumer behavior and consumer lifestyle. At the micro level, it mainly tends to explain and explain consumers' behaviors in specific information communication, purchase decision, product use, brand attitude and so on. This study is to study the behavior of online consumers at the micro level.

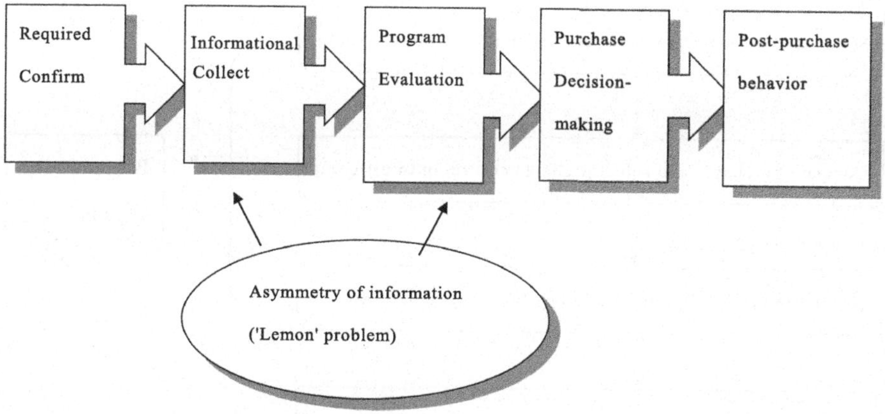

Fig. 8.1 Purchase process and 'lemon' problem

According to Kolter's 'stimulus–response' model (1994), in the purchase decision-making process of online consumers, the second and third stages of the purchase process, that is, in the information collection stage and the scheme evaluation stage, will face the problem of information asymmetry (its influence is shown in Fig. 8.1). For example, in the information collection stage, the quality of the obtained information depends on the source and quality of the information. In the program evaluation stage, the consumer evaluation criteria depend on the accumulated information of individuals and the sense of identity with brand signals. Therefore, the study of consumer behavior or marketing will inevitably encounter the problem of information asymmetry. Although Kolter's analysis is aimed at the physical market, the basic idea it reflects is also applicable to the Internet market.

8.1.2 The Information Asymmetry in the Purchase Process

Kalakota and Whinston [2] analyzed the purchase decision-making process of online consumers from the perspective of customers. The whole process is divided into three parts (see Fig. 8.2). It can be seen from this process that whether consumers purchase online depends on the type of products and the potential risks of consumers. The potential risks of consumers are related to the uncertainty of Internet product quality. Among them, the quality uncertainty determines the degree of information asymmetry, that is, the degree of adverse selection. Therefore, the types of Internet products interact with the information asymmetry in the purchase process.[2]

[2] If we look at the type of product, the important factor of Amazon's success lies in the type of product. In the eyes of consumers, the risk of buying books online is small, and the uncertainty of quality is low.

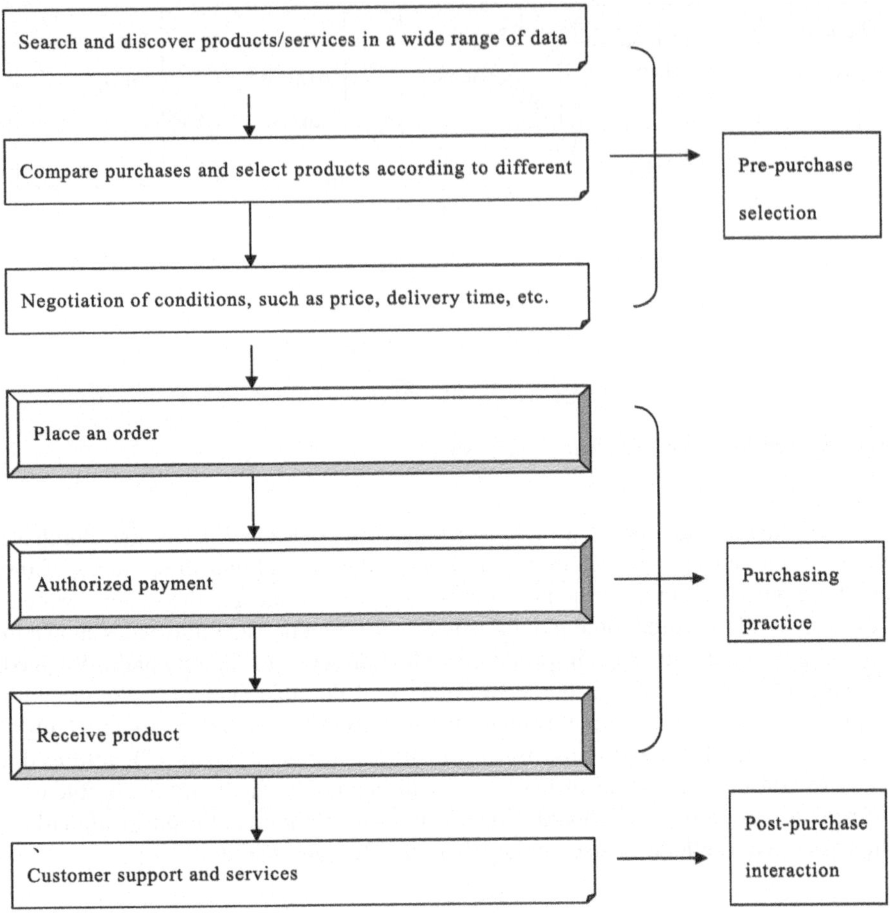

Fig. 8.2 Purchase decision process of online consumers

Iacobucci [3] also analyzed the degree of information asymmetry in the marketing process according to search, experience and trust are divided into three attributes. It lists 48 kinds of products or services, and is expressed in a continuous way. The results show that most products or services in physical form are more inclined to search, while most products or services in service form are more inclined to trust attributes. If the main attribute of a certain product or service is search attribute, customers can know the quality of the product or service before purchasing, and decide whether to buy it or not; if the main attribute of a product or service is experience attribute, customers can't know the information of the product before purchase, and only after purchase can they know the quality of the product or service; if the main attribute of a product or service is trust attribute, customers can't know the quality of the product or service after purchasing the product or service. Therefore, when evaluating, customers will rely on different criteria according to different service attributes. Internet consumers are more inclined to search attributes, while they are more cautious about items that depend on trust and experience attributes.

Iacobucci's analysis tells us that compared with the purchasing decision-making process of consumers, the difference between online shopping stage and traditional shopping stage is mainly manifested in the different attributes of products and services. And this is related to the asymmetry of information: because the quality of goods that need trust and experience attributes can only be known through experience and actual use by consumers, even if a large number of advertisements and product information are not enough to convince consumers of their quality, consumers will not buy them. Customers may take a risk if they know that quality is beneficial to future purchases, but if they only use a product once, the risk is very small. This feature also makes manufacturers have no good way to convince consumers of the quality of their products.

8.1.3 Conclusion

Compared with the physical market, an important task for consumers to engage in trading activities in the Internet market is to recognize the Internet information space. Consumers' online transactions can be described as browsing and searching related commodity information under the condition of information technology in order to complete shopping or related tasks, so as to provide necessary information for purchasing decisions and practice purchasing decisions and behaviors.

Through the analysis of the existing marketing theory, whether it is online shopping or shopping in the physical market, the shopping process and the attributes of the purchased products are related to the information asymmetry. As long as it involves the comparison of product quality and price, consumers must face the problem of adverse selection, but the Internet market is more special. In the process of online transactions, consumers' cognitive activities of Internet information space are special in that they need to browse and rely on the information environment. Search is the most effective way to find new information in a given conceptual field, and find specific items in a large amount of information set and locate information. Therefore, when we study Internet marketing and related consumer behavior, we should not ignore the influence of Internet 'lemon' problem.

For China's online market, in order to reduce the adverse selection in online transactions, we must consider the acceptance degree and ability of Chinese consumers to the internet information space, and reduce the perceived risk of consumers' online shopping.

8.2 Adverse Selection and Consumer Behavior of Chinese Netizens

8.2.1 Influencing Factors of Consumer Behavior

In addition to analyzing the marketing process, we should also analyze the determinants of consumer behavior in order to study the behavior of online consumers. Keegan [4] summed up the main factors affecting consumer behavior into four aspects (As shown in Table 8.1).

We can divide the above four aspects into external determinants and personal determinants. External determinants include cultural influence, social influence and family influence. Personal determinants include life cycle stage, occupation, income, lifestyle, personality, self-concept and psychological factors. The combination of these various factors will have an effect on consumers' purchasing behavior. To study the particularity of Chinese consumer behavior, we should especially consider these factors.

At present, the study of Chinese consumers' localization has been paid more and more attention. Many scholars are looking for theories and methods suitable for Chinese consumers' social and cultural psychology, and studying the unique behavior patterns of Chinese consumers. From the present situation, the research on Chinese consumer behavior is still at a relatively early stage, and most of the researchers come from Hong Kong and Taiwan, including the research on consumer lifestyle [5], the research on Chinese consumer research methods [6], and the comparative research on consumers in mainland China, Hong Kong and Taiwan.

Table 8.1 Main factors affecting consumer behavior

Factor category	Factor content
Cultural factors	Culture Subculture: Country, Religion, Ethnicity, Geography Social class: occupation, income, wealth, education, values
Social factors	Reference Groups: Primary, Secondary, Worship Family: Parents, children Role and Status: Identity in Different Families, Clubs and Organizations
Psychological factors	Cognition: Selective attention and selective memory Learning: Restriction, Categorization and Discrimination Beliefs Motivation
Personal factors	Age and Life Cycle Occupation Economic type Lifestyle Personality and self-concept

Source Keegan [4]

Regarding the behavior characteristics of Chinese consumers, Dai Yuanchen and Shifen Wu [7] pointed out that the growth of Chinese residents' consumption has the characteristics of convergence, which is embodied in the 'synchronous resonance' effect on the demand for high-grade durable consumer goods. Although due to the widening income gap, the phenomenon of consumption resonance is weakening, and residents' consumption begins to pursue 'individuation'. However, the social herd mentality formed by 'demonstration effect' and 'comparison effect' makes consumption resonance still have its social psychological foundation. Zhang Ping (8) believes that the risks faced by Chinese consumers are increasing. The increasing uncertainty in the future has become a prominent problem now. Long Zhihe (9) The consumption behavior of Chinese consumers is based on the pursuit of utility maximization.

Yi Zhihong [10] once summarized the behavior of Chinese consumers into five main characteristics: (1) dependence on advertising. Among them, commercial sources play the role of information notification, while non-commercial sources play the role of information verification and evaluation. On the one hand, it is due to the shortage of public information sources and empirical information sources, on the other hand, it is due to the prominent role played by advertisements in commercial information sources. (2) Worship of foreign goods and famous brands. Consumers' worship of foreign goods comes from two reasons: First, psychological reasons, for showing off, showing off and other motives, think that buying and using foreign goods can show economic strength. Second, the quality of goods. The overall situation in the market is that the quality of foreign goods is higher than that of domestic goods. (3) Pursuit of consumption hotspots. Popularity is a universal phenomenon in the world, but it has a deeper cultural and economic foundation in China. Herd mentality is a reflection of Chinese traditional behavior. The 'golden mean' advocated by traditional behavior is reflected in the consumer behavior, that is, the consumer psychology of 'following the crowd'. (4) Contradictory psychology of price reaction. In the actual purchase decision-making, consumers often take chances and try to get higher profits from lower prices. On the other hand, it is believed that 'high price and high quality must be excellent', and the result is to give some illegal traders an opportunity. (5) Lack of self-protection ability. Due to the imperfect legal system, consumers face a large number of infringements and lack of legal protection basis; due to the weak power of consumers, the consumer protection movement has not yet formed momentum, consumer protection organizations lack the necessary authority and the supervision of mass media has not formed enough pressure on enterprises.

8.2.2 Causes of Adverse Selection in China's Internet Market

Although the above research is for traditional market transactions, some characteristics still exist in online transactions, some characteristics can be maintained, some can be strengthened and some are new characteristics. The reasons are not only social and traditional factors, but also the influence brought by Internet characteristics.

As far as China's Internet market is concerned, the 'lemon' problem has special reasons besides the reasons mentioned in the previous chapters of this paper: (1) Limited acceptance of Internet information space. This mainly comes from the limitation of technical conditions and the level of cultural quality, which will unconsciously weaken the trust of netizens in online products and strengthen the degree of adverse selection of Chinese netizens. (2) The psychological reasons of worshiping foreign famous brands reduce the cognitive process of domestic product quality. (3) The consumption psychology of 'following the crowd' in Chinese traditional behavior will make it difficult for some brands to transmit quality signals, and strengthen the 'lemon' problem in Chinese online market. (4) The negative demonstration effect of some non-standard websites. In 2001, my8848, a well-known e-commerce website in China, was warned by the industrial and commercial departments that it would have an adverse impact on consumers' psychology because it was reported that it received payment for goods ordered by consumers but refused to deliver goods and the quality was inconsistent with the price. (5) The rampant counterfeiting has also strengthened the distrust of Chinese netizens on Internet products. (6) The imperfect legal system and the weak power of consumers make some online enterprises strengthen their own information advantages and reduce consumers' right to know intentionally or unintentionally, so the adverse selection faced by consumers is more serious.

8.2.3 Data and Description

According to the 49th Statistical Report on Internet Development in China (2020/7) published by China Internet Information Center,[3] online users think that the biggest problems existing in online transactions at present are: product's quality is not guaranteed (40.0%), security is not guaranteed (25.1%), payment is inconvenient (9.9%), delivery is not timely (7.1%), price is not attractive enough (10.3%), information provided online is unreliable (7.0%) and others (0.6%). Among them, the severity of the quality problem is the greatest, which shows that most consumers have different degrees of skepticism about the quality of Internet products.

[3] http://www.cnnic.cn/.

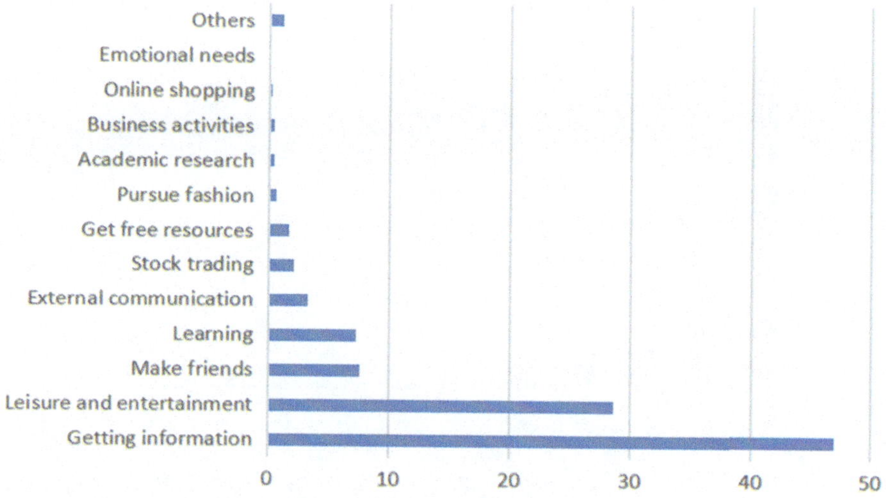

Fig. 8.3 The main purpose of netizens surfing the Internet

The survey results also show that in terms of the purpose of netizens surfing the Internet, obtaining information ranks first, and the number of netizens who choose this purpose of surfing the Internet accounts for 46.9%; followed by leisure and entertainment (accounting for 28.6%); making friends and studying in the third and fourth places accounted for more than 7% respectively; there are far fewer people who choose other online purposes (as shown in Fig. 8.3), and only 0.2% of them shop online.

By comparing the online behaviors of Chinese netizens in the past three times, we can see that the proportion of netizens who take obtaining information as the main purpose of surfing the Internet has been far ahead, accounting for about half of netizens. However, the proportion of online trading activities is relatively small, and its range hovers between 0.1% and 0.3%. This fact also illustrates the existence of the 'lemon' problem in China's online market and its serious impact (see Fig. 8.4).

In addition, by sorting out the statistics made by the Center's Statistical Report on Internet Development in China[4] for 47 consecutive years, we can find that users' concern for the quality of Internet products has been high (see Fig. 8.5), among which the highest statistical result reached 57% in January 1999, and although it declined in the middle year, it has a recent upward trend, reaching 40% in July 2020.

In 2004, China Internet Information Center conducted a sample survey on the aspects that should be improved in online shopping. In the published 'China Internet Hotspot Analysis Report', the distribution of aspects that users think should be

---

[4] Since October 1997, China Internet Network Information Center (CNNIC) has published the Survey and Statistics Report on Internet Development in China for 47 times, and there are 40 user surveys related to the quality of network products.

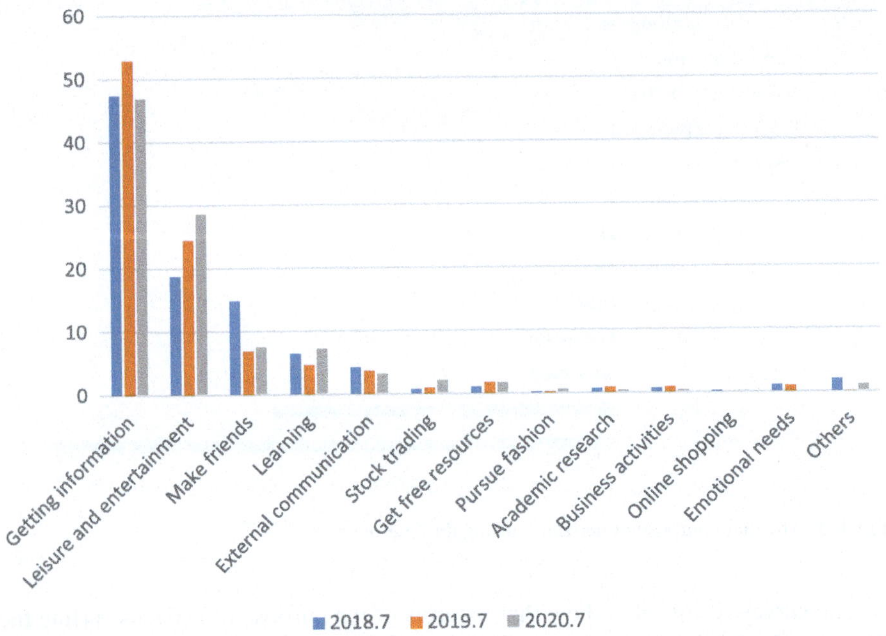

Fig. 8.4 Comparison of the last three surveys on the purpose of Chinese netizens surfing the Internet

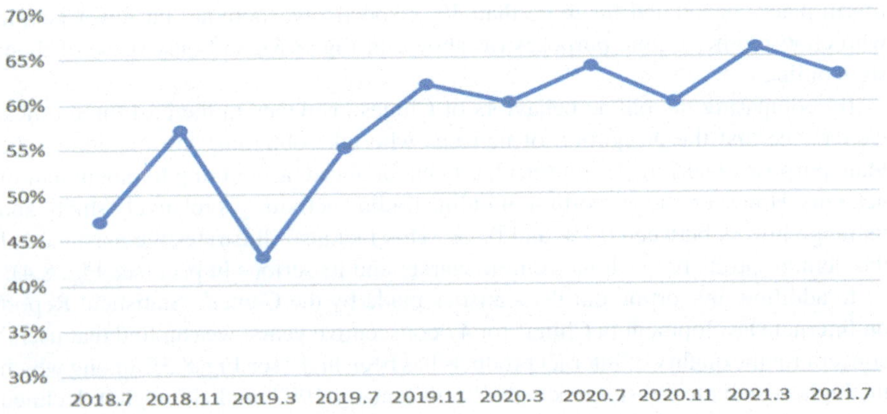

Fig. 8.5 The degree of concern of Chinese netizens for the quality of Internet products[5]

improved in online shopping is shown in Fig. 8.6. Commodity quality, delivery timeliness, information description, payment means and honesty are the most mentioned aspects. Among them, the quality of goods is mentioned most by consumers.

[5] Source: According to China Internet Network Information Center (CNNIC) Statistical Report on Internet Development in China, 2022.

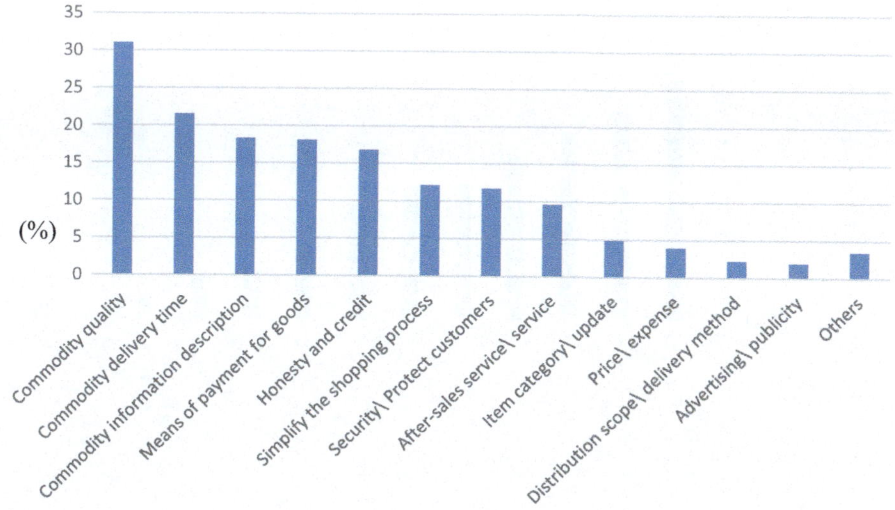

Fig. 8.6 Internet consumers think that the distribution of aspects should be improved[6]

In addition, the center also conducted a survey on the behavior of existing netizens, and the results show that the consumption behavior of existing netizens will also affect netizens who have no online purchase experience. In Fig. 8.7, we can see that among the netizens who have no purchase experience, the main reason for not trying online shopping is distrust of websites, and worrying about the quality of goods ranks second.

According to the satisfaction evaluation of each link and the analysis of selection factors, the satisfaction-importance matrix established by China Internet Network Information Center 'China Internet Network Hotspot Analysis Report' shows that the links that need to be improved urgently are commodity quality and delivery timeliness with higher importance and lower satisfaction evaluation. From the perspective of the types of goods that buyers think are important and satisfied, online shopping has certain advantages over traditional shopping methods in terms of the types of goods. The buyer satisfaction index is relatively high in terms of accurate orders, convenient inquiry and timely information feedback, which shows that after years of shopping development, the technology and service level of online merchants have also been continuously improved. In the eyes of buyers, page design, price and after-sales service are also places that online merchants need to pay attention to and improve.

[6] Source: China Internet Network Information Center (CNNIC), China Internet Hotspot Analysis Report, 2022.

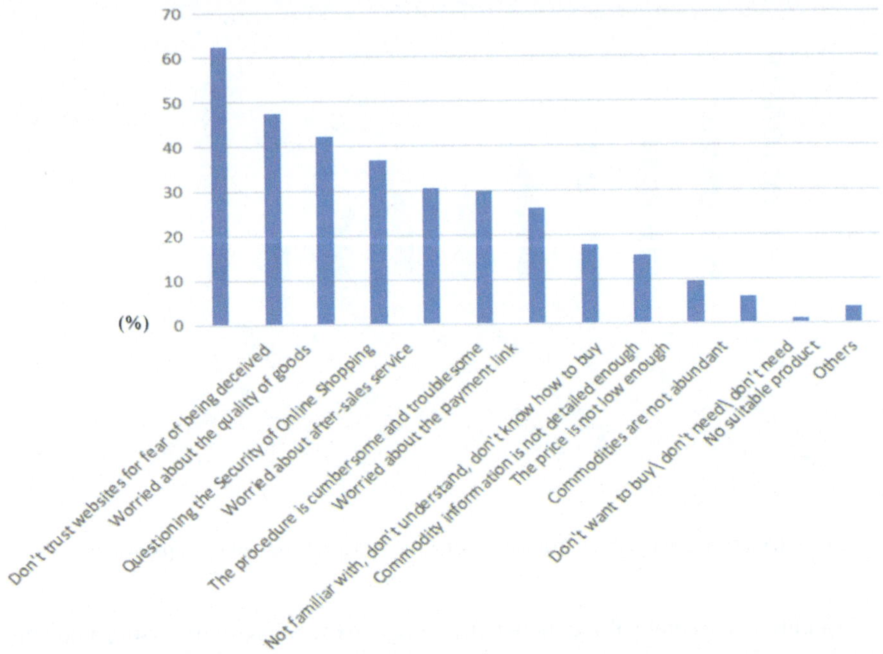

Fig. 8.7 Distribution of Reasons for Not Attempting Online Shopping[7]

The above data shows that the 'lemon' problem on the Internet in China is still serious, which must arouse our attention (Fig. 8.8).

8.3 Strategic Orientation and Countermeasures and Suggestions

The adverse selection problem in China's online market requires us to put forward countermeasures and suggestions based on the current situation of online transactions and online consumption in China and combined with the general theories and methods discussed in this paper. Therefore, the content of this section is not only for this chapter, but also for the full text.

[7] Source: China Internet Network Information Center (CNNIC), China Internet Hotspot Analysis Report, 2022.

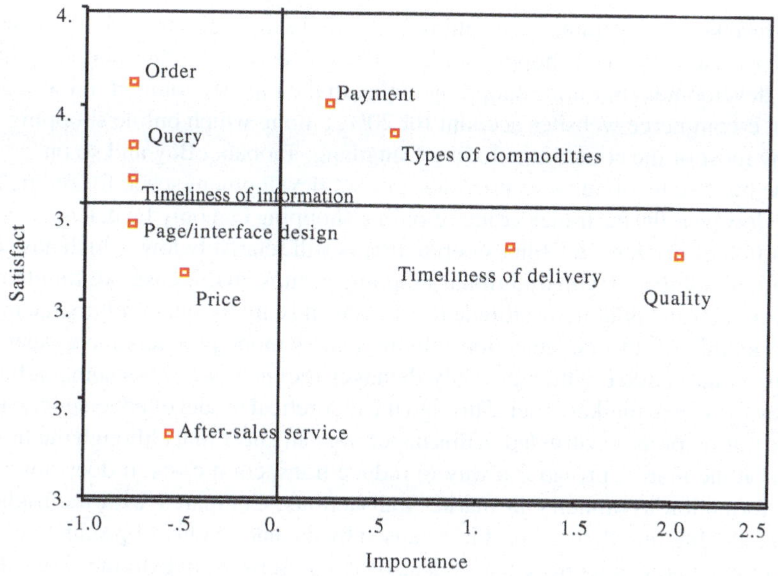

Fig. 8.8 Satisfaction-Importance Matrix[8]

8.3.1 Fully Understand the Influence of Adverse Selection on the Development of E-Commerce

The first online transaction in the world was completed in 1994,[9] while China only ushered in the first online transaction in 1998. So far, e-commerce has gone through more than five years of wind and rain in China. During these five years, the development of e-commerce in China has experienced an unhealthy and irrational management mode from circling money and burning money, paying attention to sales but not considering profits, to a rational stage. At present, China's e-commerce is in an immature to gradually mature development process.

With the popularity of the Internet, online shopping is becoming more and more popular. According to the data of the 14th China Internet Development Survey (CNNIC), as of June 2004, the number of Internet users in China has reached 87 million, accounting for about 6% of the national population. Among the 87 million netizens, 49.2% sometimes or often visit online shopping malls or shops, and 7.3% of them often use online shopping; in addition, in the last year, 37.8% of netizens used to shop online. In terms of advantages of online shopping, CNNIC survey found that 46.8% of users think it can save time, 44.9% think it can save money, 41.1% think

[8] Source: China Internet Network Information Center (CNNIC), China Internet Hotspot Analysis Report, 2004.

[9] Source: http://www.people.com.cn/GB/it/1065/2722711.html.

it is convenient to operate, 33.9% think it can find scarce goods, and 19.4% think it can experience fun when shopping online. The prosperity of online shopping has led to the development of online shopping malls. In the top 100 commercial websites in China, e-commerce websites account for 20%, among which online shopping malls occupy most of the country, including Dangdang, Taobao, eBay and so on.

The huge scale of netizens provides a broad development space for online shopping. However, the customer group of online shopping can only be netizens, and the proportion of netizens in China's population is still relatively low, which has certain limitations compared with traditional shopping groups. In this case, we should have a more rational and pragmatic attitude to regulate and care for our e-commerce market. The principle of adverse selection tells us that 'lemon' products have destructive effects on the market, which not only damages the interests of consumers, but also destroys a normal market order. Through the theoretical model of adverse selection in online transactions constructed in this paper, we can know that although the Internet-based online market provides a way to reduce transaction costs, it does not change the information asymmetry in market transactions. Compared with the traditional market, the Internet 'lemon' problem caused by the uncertainty of product quality in the Internet market not only exists, but also is more serious. In extreme cases, if there are more inferior products in the e-commerce market, the possibility of the whole transaction disintegration will be greater.

Therefore, reducing or reducing adverse selection in the Internet market is of great significance for standardizing and developing China's e-commerce market, establishing online traders' confidence in China's Internet market and increasing Chinese netizens' trust in the quality of Internet products. While we are intoxicated with the convenience of modern Internet technology, we can't ignore the information asymmetry brought by Internet virtuality and the Internet 'lemon' problem caused by it. This is the premise that we can't ignore when observing, utilizing and developing e-commerce.

8.3.2 Technical Means Should Obey the Creation of Value Chain

The use of modern Internet technology for marketing, although it can be difficult to achieve in the traditional marketing or cannot achieve marketing means, such as the Internet market characteristics of price discrimination and product customization, its advantage lies in its product price can be established on the user's evaluation, can better meet the needs of customers, to achieve 'one-to-one marketing' and other pricing strategies. However, through the analysis of the price behavior of online products, we find that they play a very limited role in solving the adverse selection problem, because this method will contain strong subjective evaluation and quality preference of sellers, which will cause huge price difference of products with the same quality, which will aggravate the information disadvantage faced by consumers on product quality. To change the adverse selection faced by online consumers, online enterprises must break through the thinking path with sales as the sole purpose, and must take the lifelong value of customers as the goal of enterprises. Value chain should be regarded as a series of technological processes in which some groups work together to create value for customers. At present, Internet marketing is still in its infancy, and many enterprises focus on improving the speed of surfing the Internet and ensuring Internet security. Undeniably, it is very important to solve these technical problems, but many enterprises also ignore the business strategy.

We should make it clear that although e-commerce based on modern Internet technology has changed the rules of operation and competition, it has not changed the reasons for the survival of enterprises. Customers' satisfaction and willingness to buy are still the focus of enterprise competition.

8.3.3 Implement the Organic Combination of Internet Marketing and Traditional Marketing

Through analysis, this study thinks that the effective solution to the 'lemon' problem in the traditional market will encounter new difficulties in the e-commerce market. Therefore, in order to reduce the 'lemon' phenomenon in the Internet market, we must emphasize the organic combination of online marketing and traditional marketing. For example, although it is difficult to reduce the 'lemon' problem by using the method of judging quality by price in the traditional market in the online market, we can use the traditional way of word-of-mouth communication to enhance customer loyalty to the Internet.

The success of Internet strategy lies not only in the skills of Internet sales, but also in the attraction of value proposition and the radiation and influence of word-of-mouth communication it stimulates.

In fact, although Internet marketing, as a new marketing concept and strategy, has formed a huge impact on the traditional management mode of enterprises. However, Internet marketing cannot completely replace traditional marketing. Up to now, the e-commerce market on the Internet is only a part of the whole commodity market, and it only occupies a small part of the whole market transaction amount from the perspective of the transaction amount of the e-commerce market. At the same time, it should be pointed out that the marketing activities are faced with spiritual people, and the Internet is only a tool, so the unique affinity of the traditional people-oriented marketing strategy cannot be replaced by Internet marketing. Internet marketing and traditional marketing are a process of integration. Internet marketing and traditional marketing will influence each other, complement each other and promote each other until they finally realize the internal unity of mutual integration in the future.

When analyzing the characteristics of Internet reputation, this paper has come to the conclusion that in order to establish the reputation of products, Internet enterprises need to recognize their own 'reputation chain' and implement the strategy of 'reputation transfer' when necessary. For the primary stage of e-commerce market in China, we should pay special attention to and make use of this point. Online companies should lengthen their 'reputation chain' and use their reputation and brand in the physical market as a 'stepping stone' to enter e-commerce.

The Internet development strategy of Lenovo Computer Company provides us with beneficial enlightenment. Lenovo Computer[10] Company is a subsidiary of Lenovo Group. Its products mainly include servers, business computers and home computers. On May 1, 2000, Lenovo Group Co., Ltd. announced that Lenovo had completed the acquisition of IBM's global personal computer business, which marked the birth of the third largest personal computer enterprise in the world. Lenovo, as a pioneer in China's IT industry, has adopted a marketing strategy of actively embracing the Internet when facing the impact of the Internet. The company used its tremendous influence in the offline market to implement the strategic shift to the Internet. E-commerce system is an important strategy and first measure for its transformation. That is, Lenovo not only provides products to sellers, but also provides high-speed and efficient business operation services.

E-commerce system will further strengthen the integration of 'Big Lenovo' in business operation, and Lenovo also plans to assist agents in the construction of their own information systems to jointly improve the business operation of both parties. Secondly, it is to establish distribution channels in the Internet age. Lenovo has opened an e-commerce system and an information management system specially used for specialty stores. The use of the Internet has improved the market adaptability of 'Big Lenovo' and enhanced the competitiveness of 'Big Lenovo'. Consumers can visit Lenovo's e-commerce website for online information inquiry, online ordering and online information communication. At the same time, the opening of e-commerce greatly simplifies the workflow, and because it avoids the error caused by manual entry, it makes the business operation process smoother (Fig. 8.9).

Similarly, the Internet marketing implemented by Haier Group is also a successful example of 'reputation transfer' strategy. Haier Group is famous for its high-quality service. In the eyes of Chinese people, 'Haier' is synonymous with high-quality products. Haier Group, an invisible gold-lettered signboard, makes it handy in the process of Internet marketing, and gives full play to the advantages of Haier Group's 'one person and two internet' (famous brand, distribution Internet and payment Internet). The group highlights this point in website construction: always put the needs and interests of customers first. In its online store, in addition to the regular recommended products and product customization, 'Your problem is our development topic!' 'As long as you can think of, we can do it' is Haier's promise. At present, dozens of domestic and foreign Internet companies are bidding for the transformation and construction scheme of websites to adapt to the next e-commerce operation. Through business process reengineering, the whole business process of the company is re-combined, and the personalization of production, sales and service is truly realized through the Internet.

[10] http://www.lcs.legend.com.cn.

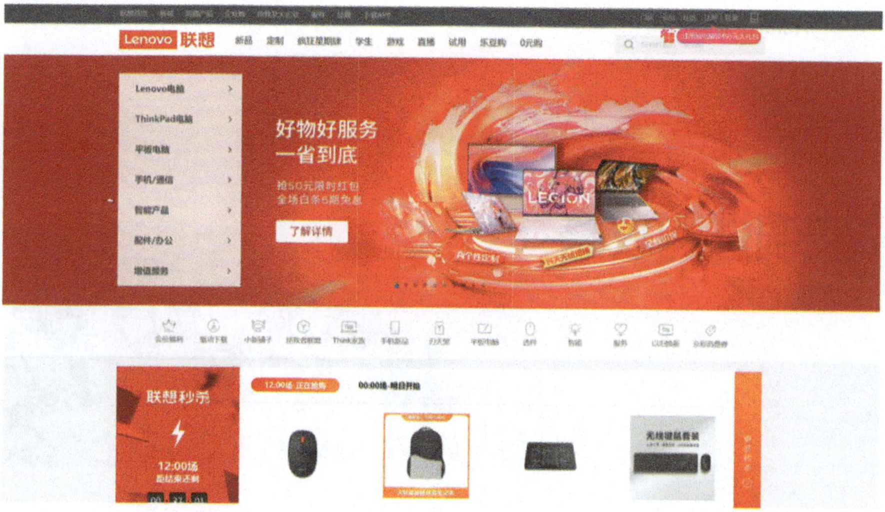

Fig. 8.9 Homepage of Lenovo computer company online mall

In addition, many enterprises in China have implemented the strategies of 'reputation transfer' and 'reputation extension'. For example, 'Nanjing Road Online' (www.sh-nanjingroad.com) and so on (Fig. 8.10).

8.3.4 Implement the Strategy of Third-Party Intervention

The basic theoretical model of this study tells us that compared with the physical market, the Internet market calls for the emergence of market coordinators more, and the use of Internet middlemen, that is, quality information brokers, in the Internet market can play a particularly important role in reducing the quality uncertainty of Internet products. Therefore, in order to create trust between buyers and sellers, it is very important to implement the strategy of third-party intervention in China's e-commerce market to ensure and improve the operational efficiency of the Internet market. By analyzing the operation mode of Internet market quality intermediary, we have proved that the mechanism of 'information spillover' of Internet intermediary will urge intermediary to maintain high-quality products. Although the participation of intermediary actually increases the transaction cost, it also increases the market efficiency. As long as the new transaction cost can increase the welfare level of the whole society, the effective intermediary will exist for a long time in the era of Internet economy.

For the development of e-commerce industry in China, we need to support and cultivate more Internet quality intermediaries, especially trustworthy quality intermediaries. At the same time, as an intermediary enterprise of Internet quality, it also needs to carefully design its system rules and strategies to ensure the correctness of

Fig. 8.10 Online mall of Haier Company[11]

product information. The case of AUCNET.COM, a Japanese used car online auction agency, provided in this paper shows that although advanced technical conditions are the necessary conditions for the success of enterprises, the innovation of systems and rules is more important (Fig. 8.11).

With the support of relevant departments and units of the State Council, China E-Commerce Association established 'China E-Commerce Integrity Alliance', aiming at strengthening the construction of China's e-commerce credit system by establishing an authoritative and fair third-party credit evaluation platform. It has 21 sponsors, including Sina, Shanda, ebay, Taobao, Yipai, Excellence, Souyide, Yunwang, Beidou Mobile Internet, Ninth City, Colorful Valley, Guangtong Communication, China Financial Certification Center and Jin Chengxin. China E-commerce Integrity Alliance is an industry standard and self-discipline organization initiated by China E-commerce Association and established by well-known e-commerce enterprises. Its aim is to stress honesty, build norms and create a safe environment for online consumption. In order to achieve this purpose, we mainly carry out four aspects of work. First, issue the credibility index, promote the logo of the integrity alliance, and second, issue the integrity convention and publish the service standards. Third, through the integrity alliance to deal with online consumer complaints, and the results of complaints will be fed back to the integrity files, and at the same time,

[11] http://www.ehaier.com.

Fig. 8.11 China E-Commerce integrity alliance web page[12]

online adjustment. Fourth, popularize and apply, and establish relevant mechanisms to protect e-commerce. In order to implement relevant work, the Alliance advocates four norms. First, the Convention of Integrity Alliance; second, the product category e-commerce service specification, the third is the service category e-commerce service specification, and the fourth, the online trading platform service specification. By standardizing and recommending excellent and honest e-commerce enterprises, the alliance protects the rights and interests of e-commerce consumers, and strives to become the code and standard of behavior of the whole e-commerce industry. We can reasonably believe that the 'Integrity Alliance' will establish an authoritative and third-party qualification and credit evaluation platform among e-commerce traders, e-commerce operators and their users, and international e-commerce operators.

8.3.5 *Give Full Consideration to China's National Conditions*

The seriousness and particularity of the 'lemon' problem in China's online market require us to fully consider China's national conditions when exploring ways to solve this problem. When analyzing the relationship between consumer behavior and adverse selection of Chinese netizens, this paper pointed out that due to the limitation of technical conditions and the influence of cultural quality, Chinese netizens' acceptance of Internet information space is still limited. Therefore, in order to

---

[12] https://www.bcpcn.com/.

reduce adverse selection in online transactions, we must fully consider the acceptance and ability of Chinese consumers to innovation, and design an Internet model that conforms to China's national conditions and characteristics:

First of all, innovation should be combined with compatibility. For a long time, people have been used to the traditional way of buying when shopping, from touching eyes to finally deciding the process of buying. If customers are required to abandon this method completely and change to decide shopping from the images and text instructions on the screen, it will be difficult for customers to adapt for a while. Therefore, we should try our best to provide consumers with the consistency between online shopping and traditional shopping experience, and consider more payment methods that are more in line with China's national conditions, such as mail payment and cash on delivery.

Secondly, improve the security of online transactions. For example, we should guarantee unconditional return within a certain period of time, so as to reduce the perceived risk of consumers' online shopping and increase their interest in trying. In addition, by setting up columns such as Help, we can answer the relevant questions that consumers may encounter in time. Cash flow is an important part of online shopping. CNNIC's previous survey data show that in China, the proportion of online payment by bank card has increased year by year, from 15.6% at the end of 2001 to 37.9% in June 2004, as shown in Fig. 3.26. However, because the profit problem between merchants and banks and the problem of bank payment cards have not been fundamentally solved, cash flow is still one of the current problems in online shopping (Fig. 8.12).

Benign competition in the industry is the foundation to promote the development and progress of the industry. The competition in the banking industry makes

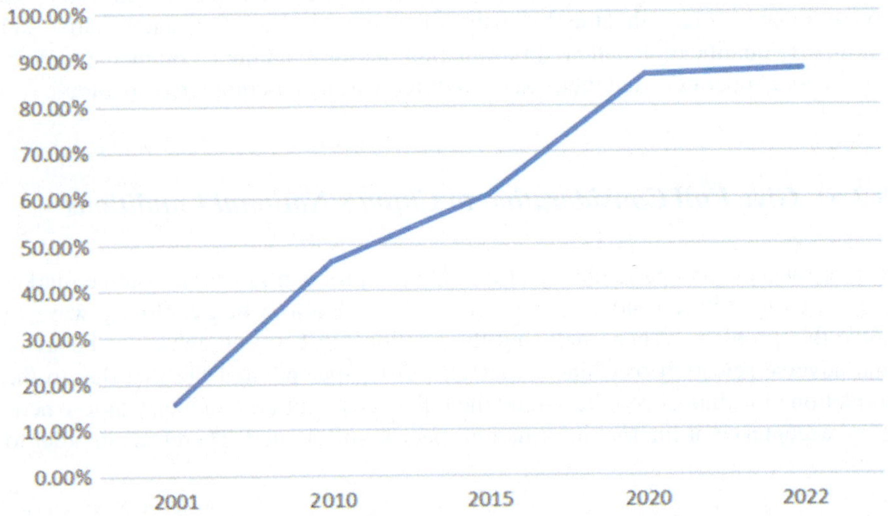

Fig. 8.12 Proportion of online payment for online shopping

bank customers get better service. In online shopping, merchants will choose a bank with better service and lower cost than the payment bank account chosen by customers. Once this problem is fundamentally solved, the transaction volume and transaction volume of online shopping will greatly increase, thus promoting the scale development of online shopping.

Third, increase convenience and reduce complexity. At present, many online stores are concentrated in large and medium-sized cities with relatively developed economy, mainly considering the distribution problem. Although the problem of commodity distribution in China has been improved, it is mainly concentrated in large and medium-sized cities, and some small cities still adopt relatively backward transportation modes, such as bicycles, which will make the last link of distribution relatively slow. In order to solve this problem, online shopping should develop in the direction of localization and regionalization. For example, some online stores solve the distribution problem by cooperating with local traditional shoppers or opening convenience stores by themselves, so as to achieve complementary advantages.

Fourth, more patterns and signs should be used to help consumers learn and understand the interactive interface quickly. Figure 8.13 shows us the shopping guide interface of JD online shopping mall, which is fast, convenient and easy for consumers to master. Online shopping is a new thing. For people who are used to traditional shopping, it takes a long time to accept this way, and it also needs the publicity and guidance of the media to cultivate people's habit of online shopping. The initial shopping action needs users' personal experience, and shopping websites need to simplify and fool the online shopping operation process, so as to reduce the difficulty and psychological barriers of customers' online shopping. When netizens have the habit of online shopping, it is not easy to change.

8.3.6 Get Out of the Misunderstanding of Internet Marketing

At present, China's Internet marketing is still in the developing stage, many people and many enterprises have some misunderstandings about Internet marketing, which need to be corrected in practice.

Some enterprises think that Internet enterprises can use Internet tracking technology and data mining technology to analyze the historical data of consumers, so as to find out the demand and implement targeted marketing strategies. Therefore, many enterprises put forward to change the past mass and large-scale production mode into customized mode according to the requirements of customers, and provide customers with personalized products and services. Undeniably, this kind of targeted marketing strategy can better meet the needs of customers and attract more customers. However, the implementation effect of this marketing strategy will also be affected by Internet adverse selection. The case of Amazon.com's price discrimination experiment failure provided by this study shows that one-sided emphasis on personalized marketing cannot effectively improve the competitive ability of enterprises, and enterprises

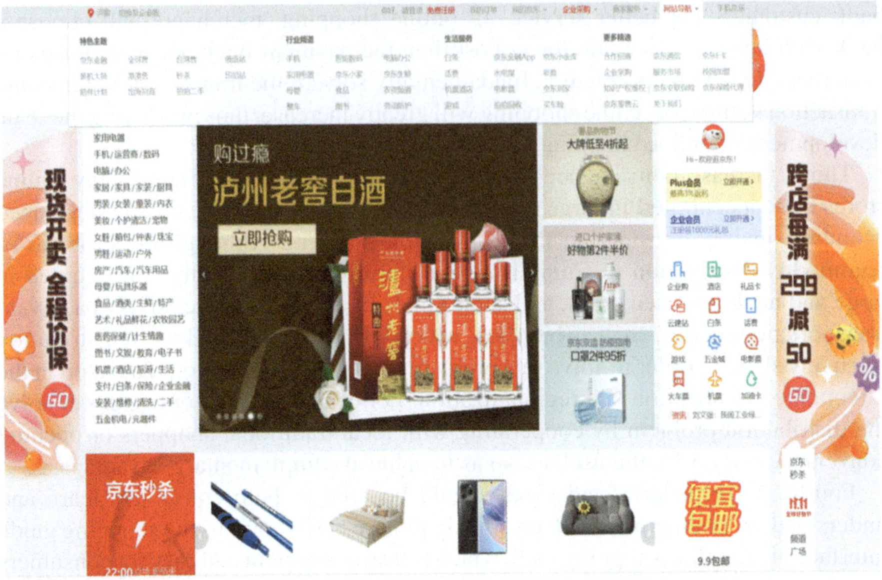

Fig. 8.13 JD shopping guide interface of online mall[13]

should make use of the interactive characteristics of the Internet to better understand customers and markets.

Some enterprises believe that the key to Internet brand building is Internet advertising. Through the research on the operation mode of Internet reputation, this paper thinks that although the entry of Internet market has a low entry barrier, because the foundation for manufacturers to obtain reputation is based on the repeated purchase of consumers, it may be more difficult for online products' brands and advertisements to be the guarantee of product quality than the physical market, and online enterprises should make use of the characteristics of physical market to make up for the disadvantages faced in the Internet market. Therefore, online enterprises must realize the characteristics of online advertising. If you just put those non-targeted e-mail advertisements directly into consumers' mailboxes, the result will only attract consumers' resentment. Now, many enterprises simply move advertising information to the Internet and 'wait for a rabbit' on the Internet, which obviously won't work. Enterprises must use traditional media to publicize their websites and web pages in order to achieve the purpose of advertising and eliminate the adverse selection faced by online consumers.

Other enterprises believe that online consumers are only sensitive to price, and only price advantage can win consumers. But the Internet 'lemon' principle tells us that because of the existence of Internet 'lemon', the price of Internet products, as a signal of product quality, plays a limited role in the Internet market. To solve the

[13] http://www.8848.net.cn/.

fundamental problem, we should also take advantage of the Internet characteristics and adopt various ways to improve consumers' loyalty and satisfaction to Internet products.

8.3.7 Provide Legal and Institutional Guarantee for Solving Internet Adverse Selection

Solving adverse selection requires not only economic means, but also non-economic means. This paper analyzes the role of non-economic means in solving Internet adverse selection, and emphasizes their functions. As far as China is concerned, to provide legal and institutional protection for online transactions, we should focus on the similarities and differences between the new transaction mode of e-commerce and the traditional transaction mode, base ourselves on the dual requirements of economic progress and consumption justice, eliminate or reduce the adverse effects brought by information asymmetry, and better protect the interests of market participants.

At present, China's legislation on e-commerce is not perfect, so it is very important to eliminate and reduce adverse selection by means of administrative and institutional means. We can learn from the way of The Federal Trade Commission (FTC), accept complaints from online consumers, formulate corresponding administrative measures, standardize the behavior of online manufacturers and give advice and warnings to consumers. On the other hand, commercial organizations with poor goodwill and fraudulent behavior, including Internet quality intermediaries, should have certain punishment measures. For commercial organizations that have committed serious fraud, their business licenses shall be revoked.

In terms of legal means, although China's laws such as Consumer Protection Law, Price Law, Product Quality Law and Contract Law have certain protection functions for consumers in obtaining high-quality products and reducing consumers' adverse selection, the relevant clauses are only for the physical market. In the case of e-commerce, it should have different characteristics from the traditional market, which requires us to carry out in-depth exploration. It is gratifying that the promulgation of the Regulations on Electronic Transactions in Guangdong Province has made a good start in this respect, but on the whole, compared with the rapid development of global e-commerce legislation, China's actions in this respect are still quite slow. We must consider the formulation of e-commerce norms in China from the perspective of globalization, and pay attention to tracking the international development trend.

Finally, it should be pointed out that the strategic orientation and countermeasures need the cooperation of ethical and cultural environment. As this paper points out when analyzing the role of non-economic means, trust, as the recognition and acceptance of a social order, plays an irreplaceable role in solving the Internet 'lemon' problem. Therefore, establishing the trust mechanism of e-commerce market and promoting the mutual trust and understanding among the participants in the Internet market are also very important issues in the development of the Internet economy in China at present, and we should pay enough attention to this issue.

References

1. Kolter (1994) Marketing Management, Analysis, Planning Implementation, and Control. 8th, Prentice Hall, Inc
2. Kalakota R, Whinston AB (1996) Frontier, Electronic Commerce. Addison-Wesley Longman Inc, Massachusetts
3. Iacobucci D (1992) An empirical examination of some basic tenets in services: Goods-services continua. Adv Serv Mark Manag 1:23–52
4. Keegan WJ (1999) Global Marketing Management, 6th edn. Prentice-Hall, Upper Saddle River, NJ
5. Yau OHM (1994) Consumer behavior in China: Consumer satisfaction and cultural value. Routledge, London and New York
6. Yang Z (1997) How to study Chinese people. Laurel Book Co., Ltd, Taipei, China
7. Dai Y, Wu S (2001) Institutional change factors in the formation of consumer demand function. Econ Trends 9:19–22
8. Zhang Ping (1999) Analysis on 'Electronic Creation'. Intellectual Property Rights (03):11–14
9. Long Zhihe (2000) Estimation of resident income in China. Journal of Southwest Jiaotong University (Social Science Edition) (1):39–42
10. Yi Z (1996) A brief analysis of Chinese consumer behavior characteristics. China's Circ Econ 2:13–15

Prospect of Future Research Work

Generally speaking, my existing research work mainly focuses on two aspects: First, model research. This paper constructs the Internet Akerlof model, and constructs other related models, such as reputation operation model and quality intermediary operation model. Another aspect is the application and countermeasure research. Based on the basic ideas and conclusions of the theoretical model, this paper discusses how to reduce or eliminate Internet adverse selection. Although I have made my best efforts, these studies are only staged, and there are still many problems that need further analysis and discussion—these problems are also the direction of my further research:

1. Continue to deepen the Internet 'lemon market' model. In the previous work, I studied the Internet Akerlof model based on the difference of product quality preferences between market participants, but the influence of Internet structure on this model has not been included in the research perspective. The next research will focus on the influence of Internet market structure on this model. R. Albert and A-L. Barab á si published the Scale-free Internets theory in 1999, which provides a new research idea and research method for this study.
2. Extension of research methods. In this paper, the mathematical model (logical model) is mainly used in the analysis process. The advantage of this method is to express all kinds of things and their attributes in the objective system with mathematical relations or logical relations. However, when there are many factors, complex relations, and many subjects with conflicting interests and many uncertain factors, it is actually difficult to sum up clear mathematical equations or logical relations. Therefore, new research methods should be tried and used.
3. Research on specific markets. In fact, each market has its own characteristics and personality. To better study the Internet 'lemon' problem, we need to study the characteristics of each market case.

Y. Pan, *Trust Management in the Chinese E-Commerce Market*, Advanced Studies in E-Commerce, https://doi.org/10.1007/978-981-97-1115-4

4. Institutional research and mechanism design. In the traditional market, we already have some good laws, regulations and systems to solve adverse selection, such as 'Lemon Law', but how to design the mechanism in the e-commerce market is still a problem that needs to be studied.
5. Research on the correlation between adverse selection and Internet technology. Although this thesis studies the adverse selection problem from the perspective of economics and management, it is impossible to study the Internet market problem completely without the technical environment of the Internet. Only by combining the two can we have a deeper understanding of the impact of electronic market on economy.

Postscript

This book is revised on the basis of my doctoral thesis, and it is also the first monograph specializing in adverse selection ('lemon' problem) in China. According to my understanding, the topic selection of a doctoral thesis should meet the following conditions: first, it should have theoretical novelty, which is the basis to ensure the innovation of the thesis; Secondly, it should have practical guidance, which is the vitality of this paper; Thirdly, the author has already had a substantial preliminary research foundation in this field, and has certain relevant achievements. The reason why I regard the adverse selection problem ('lemon' problem) in the online market as the goal of my doctoral research is mainly based on the consideration of the above reasons.

As far as the development of adverse selection theory itself is concerned, although many scholars have promoted and expanded the 'lemon market' model, they have hardly set foot in the adaptability of the traditional 'lemon market' model in the network market, and no one has made a standardized analysis of the 'lemon' problem in the network market. In addition, through long-term observation of the current situation of China's Internet, I found that the 'lemon' problem in China's Internet market is quite serious, and it may even affect the development of China's e-commerce, which requires us to put forward countermeasures and suggestions. Therefore, the study of this problem is the dual needs of theory and practice. In addition, because I have been engaged in the teaching and research of information economy and information management in colleges and universities for a long time before studying for a doctoral degree, I have already had some preliminary research and academic accumulation on this issue.

Although there are many theoretical schools of information economics, I have always been interested in Professor Akerlof's adverse selection theory and 'lemon market' model. The reason is not only that adverse selection theory is the basic analysis theory of information economics, but also that I am impressed by this master's profound insight and unparalleled theoretical analysis skills! In 2001, the first year when I entered Renmin University to study for my doctoral degree, Professor Akerlof

Y. Pan, *Trust Management in the Chinese E-Commerce Market*,
Advanced Studies in E-Commerce, https://doi.org/10.1007/978-981-97-1115-4

won the Nobel Prize in Economics, which strengthened my determination to study the 'lemon' problem on the Internet and was full of confidence in achieving the expected results.

In the course of research, I always believe that although the modern network economy is caused by Internet technology, it is not only possible but also necessary to discuss and analyze the network 'lemon' problem from the perspective of economics and management. As pointed out by Soon-Yong Choi, Dale. O. Stahl and Andrew B. Whinston of the Center for Electronic Commerce at the University of Texas at Austin in their book 'The Economics of Electronic Commerce', 'Internet provides a good way to reduce transaction costs, but its future development will mainly depend on solutions to economic problems rather than technical problems[1]'. I quite agree with this view.

It is a little gratifying that I have published more than ten academic papers on adverse selection in national authoritative journals, core journals and international academic conferences, such as Economic Trends, Scientific Research Management and Journal of Information Science. It is not only an affirmation and recognition of my research results, but also an incentive for me to continue my research.

On the verge of completing his doctoral thesis, I first thank my tutors Professor Yu Chen and Professor Meiqi Fang. In the process of writing the thesis, the two professors gave me great inspiration and help from the topic selection to the revision and finalization of the thesis. Without the careful guidance and concern of the two teachers, there would be no this paper, which condenses the painstaking efforts and expectations of the tutor! Over the past three years, they have constantly created opportunities for me to study and research, constantly guided me to broaden my horizons in the process of academic research, encouraged me to explore bravely, and provided me with useful ideas and a large number of references. From my tutor, I realized the true meaning of being a teacher, and from my tutor's academic concept, I felt a broad academic horizon. The two tutors' rigorous academic spirit, humble and peaceful scholar style, generous life standards and tireless character will benefit me all my life. In fact, before I studied for my doctoral degree, I was fortunate to get the guidance and help of Professor Yu Chen, who led me into the hall of scientific research. Here, I would like to express my lofty respect and heartfelt thanks to my teacher! In the future life, I can only repay my teacher's care with more fruitful academic achievements.

Thanks to Renmin University of China, which carefully cultivated my growth, she provided me with a rare learning opportunity and created a good humanistic environment and rich academic resources for me.

I would like to thank Professor Akerlof of the University of California, Berkeley, for his timely reply to my e-mail many times during his busy schedule. Although Professor Akerlof is a Nobel laureate in economics, I am deeply touched by his humble and earnest attitude. I would also like to thank Professor Charles A. Wilson of New York University in the United States, Professor Colin Rose of Sydney University

[1] Choi, S.Y., Stahl, D.O, and Whinston, A.B., 1997, The Economics of Electronic Commerce, Macmillan Technical Publishing, Indianapolis, p 92.

in Australia and Professor Jae-Cheol Kim of New York State University in the United States for their support to my work.

I would like to thank the experts and scholars who have given me selfless help in the process of reviewing and defending my thesis. They are: Professor Guoqing Huo from School of Management, Graduate School of Chinese Academy of Sciences; Professor Dong Li from Guanghua School of Management, Peking University; Professor Binghui Hou from Tsinghua University; Professor Fukang Fang from Beijing Normal University; Professor Renchu Gan from Beijing Institute of Technology; Professor Kongwu Kuang from Beijing University of Information Science and Technology; Professor Kejun Liu from Naval Equipment Demonstration Center; Professor Huaying Shu from Beijing University of Posts and Telecommunications.

I would like to thank my school friends Professor Kang Xie from School of Management, Sun Yat-sen University, Associate Professor Mingming Wang and Associate Professor Meiyun Zuo from Renmin University of China. I would also like to thank Famin Yi, Bo Yang, Zhongmin Xie, Hongjiao Fu, Yiliang Hu, Jiagui Zhong, Bingquan Wei, Donglai Niu, Feng Shen, Sheng Zhong, Jianguo Yang, Shuren Zhang, Qingzuo Zhou, Xiumin Ye, Weizhu Chen and Yazhi Wang. They put forward many suggestions in my thesis writing, which helped us a lot.

Yong Pan

References

1. A review of economic theories by Xiangyang Li and Nobel laureate Akerlof—on information asymmetry and market defects. Int Econ Rev 6(2001):59–61
2. Akerlof GAA (1980) Theory of social custom, of which unemployment may one consequence. Q J Econ 94:749–755
3. Akerlof GA (1983) Loyalty filters. Am Econ Rev 73:54–63
4. Arrow K (1989) Information economics. Beijing Institute of Economics Press, Beijing
5. Joseph Pine B (2000) Mass customization (trans: Yunfu Cou). Renmin University of China Press, Beijing
6. Bailey JP, Bakos Y (1997) An exploratory study of the emerging role of electronic intermediaries. Int J Electron Commer 1(3)
7. Liu B (2001) Consumer behavior under asymmetric information. Bus Econ Manage 7:18–21
8. Lv B, Zhang P (2001) 77 Innovative models of network economy. Liaoning People's Publishing House, Shenyang
9. Bond EW (1984) Test of the 'lemons' model: reply. Am Econ Rev 72:836–840
10. Brian C, Brand W (1997) Roses or lemons: adverse selection in the market for thoroughbred yearlings. Rev Econ Stat 79:521–552
11. Kahin B, Varian H (2003) Media economics-digital information economics and intellectual property rights (trans: Chang Y et al). CITIC Publishing House, Beijing
12. Carlton J, Bensigner K (2000) Phony bids put eBay on defensive. Wall Street J 24:B1 and B4
13. Engel C (1997) Control of internet content. Foreign Soc Sci 6:38–43
14. Zhang C (2000) An analysis of American electronic commerce law. Leg Sci 2:99–106
15. Huang C, He W (1998) Information economics. Economic Science Press, Beijing
16. Cooper R, Ross TW (1984) Prices, product qualities and asymmetric information: the competitive case. Rev Econ Stud 51:197–207
17. Couton C, Gardes F, Thepaut Y (1996) Hedonic prices for environment and safety characteristic and Akerlof effect in the French car market. Appl Econ Lett 3:435–440
18. Carlton D, Peroff J (1998) Modern industrial organization. Shanghai People's Publishing House, Shanghai
19. Engel JF (1978) Blackwell and Kollat, consumer behavior, 2rd edn. The Dryden Press
20. Eric Ras Miao Sen (2003) Game and information (trans: Wang HH et al). Peking University Press, Sanlian Bookstore, Beijing
21. Feinstein JS, Block MK, Nold FC (1985) Asymmetric information and collusive behavior in auction markets. Am Econ Rev 75:441–460
22. Tian F, Wan Y (2001) Summary of research on network economy. Teach Res 2:76–78
23. Biglaiser G, Ma CA (2003) Price and quality competitive under adverse selection: market organization and efficiency. RAND J Econ 34(2):266–286

Y. Pan, *Trust Management in the Chinese E-Commerce Market*,
Advanced Studies in E-Commerce, https://doi.org/10.1007/978-981-97-1115-4

24. Geng P, Lv B, Hu X (2004) Online auction and defects of reputation mechanism. Forecast 1:33–36
25. Giffin K (1967) The contribution of studies of source credibility to a theory of interpersonal trust in the communication process. Psychol Bull 68:104–120
26. Li G, Guo Z (1999) American legislation against price discrimination. Price Market 9:45–46
27. Hendel I, Lizzeri A (1999) Interfering with secondary markets. RAND J Econ 30:1–21
28. Hensher DA, Johnson LW (1981) Applied discrete choice modeling. Wiley, New York
29. Hershriver J, Riley JG (2000) Uncertainty and information analysis (trans: Liu G et al). China Social Sciences Press, Beijing
30. Wang H (2001) Evaluation of the United Nations Model Law on Electronic Commerce. Sci Technol Law Quart 1:121–122
31. Hoque AY, Lohse GL (1999) An information search cost for designing interfaces for electronic commerce. J Mark Res 26:387–394
32. Li H (2000) Methodology of management research. Xi'an Jiaotong University Press, Xi'an
33. Zhu H, Li X (2003) Review of foreign internet price research results. Foreign Econ Manage 6:45–48
34. Xiong H (2000) Research on agent-based economic model. Ph.D. Thesis of Renmin University of China
35. Sun J, Ji J (1998) On the application of price segmentation strategy in practice. Foreign Econ Manage 8:16–19
36. Jiandong W, Wu X (2001) George Akerlof's New Keynesian economic thoughts: a series of comments on the academic contributions of potential Nobel prize winners in economics. Econ Trends 3:67–71
37. Zhang J (2001) Research on the legal system of consumer protection in e-commerce. Law 11:53–55
38. Wu J (1999) E-commerce-the main trade mode in the 21st century. Finance Trade Econ 4:85–60
39. Wu J (1997) Information economics. Econ Trends 8:3–5
40. Wu J (1999) Information economy and knowledge economy. Economic Science Press, Beijing
41. Wu J (2001) Is the new economy new in software products? Discussion with Comrade Li Luoli. Econ Res 3:83–85
42. Wu J, Xie K, Wang M (2002) Information economics. Higher Education Press, Beijing
43. Wu J (2000) Network economy and its influence on economic theory. Acad Res 1:5–11
44. Wu J (1996) Network revolution and network economics. Econ Trends 11:7–10
45. Xie K (1994) A review of western micro-information economics. Econ Trends 2:68–73
46. Xie K, Yu C (1998). The origin and development of knowledge economy thought. Renmin University of China Press
47. Xie K, Xiao J, Zhao G (2003) Electronic commerce economics. Electronic Industry Press, Beijing
48. Xie K (1995) Micro information economics. Sun Yat-sen University Press, Guangzhou
49. Xie K (2000) Research on information economics abroad. Sci Decision-Making 4:41–46
50. Keeney RL (1999) The values of internet commerce to the consumer. Manage Sci 45:533–542
51. Klein B, Leffler KB (1981) The role of market forces in assuring contractual performance. J Polit Econ 89(August):615–641
52. Landon S, Smith CE (1998) Quality expectations, reputation, and price. South Econ J 64:628–647
53. Lee HG (1998) Do electronic marketplaces lower the price of goods? Comm ACM 41(1):73–80
54. Liu L (2002) Consumer behavior characteristics under information technology. J Inf Sci 2:237–241
55. Fan L (2001) Business model of information products based on network. Econ Res 10:38–45
56. Wang L (2002) Review of Chinese consumer behavior research in transitional period. Econ Trends 7:53–55

57. Lucking-Reily D (1999) Using field experiments to test equivalence between auction format: magic on the internet. Am Econ Rev 89(5):1063–1080
58. Li L, Guo J (2002) Network trust crisis and ethical and cultural environment of e-commerce. J Soc Sci Xiangtan Univ 4:7–9
59. Mayer RC, Davis JH, Schoorman FD (1995) An integrative model of organizational trust. Acad Manag Rev 20(3):709–733
60. Fang M (1999) Introduction to E-commerce. Tsinghua University Publishing House, Beijing
61. Fang M, Hu Y (2003) Network marketing. Tsinghua University Publishing House, Beijing
62. Tang M, Mao Y (2000) Frontier topics of modern economics (Part III). Commercial Press, Beijing
63. He M (2003) Internet consumption: theoretical model and behavior analysis. Heilongjiang People's Publishing House, Harbin
64. Huang M, Zhu H, Li X (2003) Review of foreign internet price research results. Foreign Econ Manage 6:45–48
65. Kotler P et al (2002) New theory of Kotler Marketing. CITIC Publishing House, Beijing
66. Pindick R, Rubenfeld D (1997) Microeconomics (Chinese Translation). Renmin University of China Press, Beijing
67. Kang P, Chen W (2000) Amazon and Merrill Lynch: the meaning between victory and failure. Economic News 27
68. Doorenbos RB, Etzioni O, Weld DS (1996) A scalable comparison-shopping agent for the world wide web. Technical report UW-CSE-96-01-03, University of Washington
69. Doorenbos RB, Etzioni O, Weld DS (1997) A scalable comparison-shopping agent for the world-wide-web. In: Proceedings of the first international conference on autonomous agents, California
70. Regulations of Guangdong Province on Electronic Transactions. http://www.jcrb.com.cn/zyw/n1/ca17329.htm. Accessed 29 Jan 2003
71. Ruddy JF (1995) Photograde: a photographic grading encyclopedia for United States coins, 18th edn. Bowers and Merna Galleries, Inc.
72. Sartan Comali (2000) Economics in the information age (trans: Yao K et al). Jiangsu People's Publishing House, Nanjing
73. Schlenker BR, Helm B, Tedeschi JT (1973) The effects of personality and situational variables on behavioral trust. J Pers Soc Psychol 25(3):419–427
74. Scotson M, Taylor K (2002) Confusion and paradox in economics (trans: Wu H et al). Huaxia Publishing House
75. Shapiro C, Varian H (1998) Information rules: a strategic guide to the network economy. Harvard Business School Press
76. Shapiro C (1983) Premiums of high quality products as returns to reputations. Quart J Econ 98(November):659–679
77. Shapiro DL, Sheppard BH, Cherakin L (1992) Business on a handshake. Negotiation J 8(4):365–377
78. Choi S-Y et al (2000) Economics of E-commerce (trans: Zhang D et al). Electronic Industry Press, Beijing
79. Stiglitz (1997) Economics. Renmin University of China Press, Beijing
80. Taylor T (1997) Of industrial organization. Renmin University of China Press, Beijing
81. Yang T (2002) Network brand and its operation. Econ Manage 3:46–49
82. Zhu T (2002) Internet market efficiency paradox: a new explanatory framework. World Economy 2:12–20
83. Vickery W (1961) Counterspeculation, auction, and competitive sealed tenders. J Finance 16:8–37
84. Weil P, Vitale MR (2001) Place to space: migrating to eBusiness model. Harvard Business School Press
85. Ge W (1989) Information economics. Shanghai People's Publishing House, Shanghai
86. Zhang W (1996) Game theory and information economics, Shanghai. Shanghai People's Publishing House, Shanghai Joint Publishing House

87. Ye W (2001) Analysis of factors affecting online consumers' buying behavior. J Tianjin Bus Sch 2:25–28
88. Williams GC (2000) Saturn dealers，eBay to link used checks. San Antonio Express News 17:20–21
89. Wrightsman LS (1972) Social psychology in the seventies. Brooks/Cole, Pacific Grove, CA
90. Ma X, Li G (2002) Ten misunderstandings of network marketing. Tech Econ Manage Res 5:98–99
91. Huang X (2002) A theoretical review of trust between enterprises. Econ Trends 10:59–64
92. Yang X (2003) Review of Chinese consumer behavior research. Economic Jingwei 1:56–58
93. Han X, Wen B, Jiang B, Wang C (2000) Business philosophy and success factors of electronic intermediary enterprises. Foreign Econ Manage 3:39–42
94. Wang X (1998) Reputation management theory and its development. Econ Trends 2:53–56
95. Chen X (1997) Game analysis of price competition decision. Foreign Econ Manage 5:8–12
96. Chen Y, Jiang Y (2000) Current situation and trend of American network economy research. Econ Trends 12:64–68
97. Pan Y (2002) Research on the'lemon' problems in the e-marketing. In: Proceedings of international conference on e-business (ICEB2002). Beijing Institute of Technology Press
98. Chen Y (1998) A course in information economics. Tsinghua University Publishing House, Beijing
99. Chen Y, Xie K (1998) Information economics and its application. Reform 2:95–101
100. Chen Y, Xie K (1998) Measurement theory and method of knowledge economy. Renmin University of China Press
101. Zhang Y (1992) Basic problems of information and information economics. Tsinghua University Publishing House, Beijing
102. Bai Y, Jing J (2003) Theory and empirical research on information commodity price. J Inf Sci 10:626–631
103. Ji Y (1998) The rise of network economy: new challenges facing economics. Econ Trends 5:3–8
104. Zarker LG (1986) Production of trust: institutional source of electronic structure, 1984–1920. Res Organ Behav 8:55–111
105. Li Z, Suilian L (2002). Research on consumer behavior in e-commerce environment. Chinese Manage Sci 6:88–91
106. Zhong W, Chen J (2000) Network effect and network externality: discussion and analysis of concepts. Contemp Econ Sci 11:13–20
107. Guo Z (2003) Research on legislation of price discrimination. J Jinan (Philosophy and Social Sciences) 5:7–13
108. Densetz, Harold, The Cost of Transacting, *The Quarterly Journal of Economics*, 1968, 33–35
109. Kolter (1994) Marketing Management, Analysis, Planning Implementation, and Control. 8th, Prentice Hall, Inc
110. Zhang Ping (1999) Analysis on 'Electronic Creation'. Intellectual Property Rights (03):11–14
111. Long Zhihe (2000) Estimation of resident income in China. Journal of Southwest Jiaotong University (Social Science Edition) (1):39–42
112. Yi Z (1996) A brief analysis of Chinese consumer behavior characteristics. China's Circ Econ 2:13–15
113. Mark Skousen Kenna C (1988) Taylor，Puzzles & Paradoxes in Economics. Edward Elgar Publishing
114. Schlenker BR, Helm B, Tedeschi JT (1973) The Effects of Personality and Situational Variables on Behavioral Trust. J Personality and Social Psychology 25(3):419–427
115. Remple JK, Holmes JG, Zanna MP (1985) Trust in close relationships. Journal of Personality and Social Psychology 49:95–112
116. Brock WA, Hommes CH (1997) A Rational Route to Randomness. Econometrica 65(5):1059–95
117. Zarker LG (1986) Production of Trust: Institutional Source of Electronic Structure,1984-1920. Research in Organizational Behavior, 8:55–111

118. Shapiro DL, Sheppard BH, Cherakin L (1992) Business On a Handshake. Negotiation Journal 8(4):365–377
119. Sako M (1992) Prices, quality, and trust:inter-firm relations in Britain and Japan. Cambridge University Press
120. Griffin J (1995) Customer Loyalty. How to Earn it and How to Keep it. Lexingtong Books, New York
121. Chow S, Reed H (1997) Toward an understanding of loyalty: the modern role of trust. J Manag Issues 9(3):275–298

The manufacturer's authorised representative in the EU is Springer Nature Customer Service Centre GmbH, Europaplatz 3, 69115 Heidelberg, Germany. If you have any concerns regarding our products, please contact ProductSafety@springernature.com

Printed and bound by CPI Group (UK) Ltd, Croydon, CR0 4YY
01/10/2026
02225875-0014